S0-AVT-460

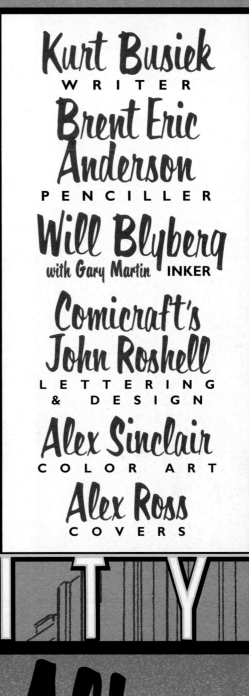

Kurt Busiek
WRITER

Brent Eric Anderson
PENCILLER

Will Blyberg
with Gary Martin INKER

Comicraft's John Roshell
LETTERING & DESIGN

Alex Sinclair
COLOR ART

Alex Ross
COVERS

Astro CITY

Family Album

Busiek, Anderson & Ross
CHAMBER OF COMMERCE

Juke Box Productions

Ann Huntington Busiek
MANAGING EDITOR

Richard Starkings
ART DIRECTOR

Jonathan Peterson	Editor – Original Series
Kristy Quinn	Editor
Jessica Chen	Assistant Editor
Robbin Brosterman	Design Director – Books
Shelly Bond	Executive Editor – Vertigo
Hank Kanalz	Senior VP – Vertigo & Integrated Publishing
Diane Nelson	President
Dan DiDio and Jim Lee	Co-Publishers
Geoff Johns	Chief Creative Officer
Amit Desai	Senior VP – Marketing & Franchise Management
Amy Genkins	Senior VP – Business & Legal Affairs
Nairi Gardiner	Senior VP – Finance
Jeff Boison	VP – Publishing Planning
Mark Chiarello	VP – Art Direction & Design
John Cunningham	VP – Marketing
Terri Cunningham	VP – Editorial Administration
Larry Ganem	VP – Talent Relations & Services
Alison Gill	Senior VP – Manufacturing & Operations
Jay Kogan	VP – Business & Legal Affairs, Publishing
Jack Mahan	VP – Business Affairs, Talent
Nick Napolitano	VP – Manufacturing Administration
Sue Pohja	VP – Book Sales
Fred Ruiz	VP – Manufacturing Operations
Courtney Simmons	Senior VP – Publicity
Bob Wayne	Senior VP – Sales

SUSTAINABLE FORESTRY INITIATIVE

Certified Chain of Custody
20% Certified Forest Content,
80% Certified Sourcing
www.sfiprogram.org
SFI-01042
APPLIES TO TEXT STOCK ONLY

Library of Congress Cataloging-in-Publication Data

Busiek, Kurt, author.
Astro City,Family Album / Kurt Busiek, writer ; Brent Anderson, artist.
pages cm
Summary: "Snapshots. They let us capture moments of truth, fragments of time -- and that's as true in Astro City, a city of heroes, villains, monsters and more, as it is anywhere. You're invited, in the Family Album, to share some of the city's greatest memories--from the wonder and terror experienced by a family new in town, to a world-famous superhero's first day at school, a crimefighter and his wife facing momentous decisions about the future, and more."-- Provided by publisher.
ISBN 978-1-4012-3531-4
1. Graphic novels. I. Anderson, Brent Eric, illustrator. II. Title. Family Album.

PN6728.A79B79 2015
741.5'973--dc23

2014046034

ASTRO CITY: Family Album, published by DC Comics, 1700 Broadway, New York, NY 10019.

Cover Copyright © 2015
Sketches and compilation © 1996 Juke Box Productions.

Originally published as Kurt Busiek's Astro City Volume 2 #1–3 and 10–13 © 1996, 1997. All Rights Reserved. Astro City, its logos, symbols, prominent characters featured in this volume and the distinctive likenesses thereof are trademarks of Juke Box Productions. VERTIGO is a trademark of DC Comics. The stories, characters and incidents featured in this publication are entirely fictional. DC Comics does not read or accept unsolicited ideas, stories or artwork.

DC Comics, 1700 Broadway, New York, NY 10019
A Warner Bros. Entertainment Company.

Printed on recyclable paper.
Printed by RR Donnelley, Salem, VA, USA. 3/16/2015. First printing
ISBN: 978-1-4012-3531-4

Dedications

To my sisters — Amy, Robin, Faith and Jennifer — who gave me a thorough grounding in family life, and to Sydney Ann, my impending daughter, who'll teach me all about it from a new perspective.

— KURT

To Sydney, Liberty, and Stone, the newest members of the Astro City family; and to Grace and Blythe Sinclair, our most colorful additions.

— BRENT

I'm so very alone.

— ALEX

Contents

Introduction

The Roses of Heliogabalus
Sir Lawrence Alma-Tadema

by Harlan Ellison

THERE WAS A SUNNY TIME, SOME YEARS AGO, when I spent whole seasons in Astro. Some PR flack out of New York had been hired to "promote" the City, and the still, silent eye of his brainstorm campaign was to drop the "City" and just refer to it as "Astro" or, even more preposterous, "the Big A."

Fortunately, its vogue was short-lived, narrow, and went nowhere reifying. And pretty soon they fired his agency, and the billboards were gone, and the cardboard stand-ups turned yellow in barbershop windows, and those with good sense dropped it; and now, the only people who call it "the Big A" are the same species of parvenus and arrivistes who call San Francisco "Frisco" or pronounce Oregon "ore-uh-gawn." But some of us still fall back on calling it Astro... when no one's looking.

Don't get over to Astro City much these days. Not since I had the quadruple bypass. Can't stand travel much—and it *is* something like twelve hundred miles from L.A.—and so I've had to postpone over and over again what used to be a fairly regular hegira: to Astro City, to hang out with Kurt and Alex and, especially, Brent, who only gets goofier with age.

But there were times when we sat, all four of us, looking out on the Raboy Esplanade, in that elegant lobby cafe (the name of which I cannot, for the life of me, remember) in the big glass-and-steel office building across from the Museum, staring at the sweep and swirl of the Deco facade, talking shop, talking art, talking superfolk and dreams, talking about all the things that pass out of one's mind half an hour beyond the brilliance of camaraderie.

Oftentimes I reminisce and am lured to the conclusion that it was the presence of the Finlay-Cartier Museum of Fine Arts that inspired us so. I can't remember similar sessions of chat with other friends, in other venues, being nearly as scintillant or filled with cheer. And so, I *miss* Astro.

Good times there, good people—even if Busiek was always *kvetching* about some deadline or other—as well as something constantly happening. And the thing that *always* amazed me was that never did I—or anyone else I talked to—feel inferior to the "powered people," what citizens of Astro called "the costumes." Oh, we'd see them all the time, here and there... but mostly over there, doing their super-business, and we were over here...doing our non-super business. But it was always sort of *never the twain shall meet.*

I'll get back to all that in a minute.

Indulge me. I want to explain why it is, for me, that Astro is a very special place, a *nidus* if you will. With an explanation, by way of metaphor.

Indulge me. It's my way. I do, after all, make my not inconsiderable living by telling stories, imparting lies, cobbling up scenarios.

AFTER A BIT, SIR LAWRENCE ALMA-TADEMA, AND THAT PAINTING on loan from some private collection in the U.K. or the Netherlands, as it hung before us, the four of us, in the West Gallery of the Finlay-Cartier, many years ago. In a moment. But first. By metaphor...

In the opening decade of the twentieth century, Gustav Stickley's *The Craftsman,* a magazine that promoted lively discussion of the arts and crafts tradition in the United States, ran a series of essays by Irene Sargent, a woman of powerful critical voice, championing the design jewelry of the incomparable René Lalique. This was prior to his glass of high art we honor today.

She referred to Lalique, early on, as a "model of ingenuity, imagination, and craftsmanship." Kurt Busiek. Brent Anderson. Alex Ross. (And, one presumes, though I don't know him, Will Blyberg. Whose inclusion in all that has gone before, and all that follows, goes without saying. Because the core cadre admits no one even an iota less ingenious, imaginative, and craftwise than itself.) She said, of Lalique, that he was the avatar of "art nouveau" (a term then applied to only the most innovative in art), whose concepts "actively challenge others to surpass his achievements by setting a creative standard on a very high plateau." Kurt Busiek. Brent Anderson, goofier by the year. Alex and Will. And finally, by metaphor, this: "Taken thus for all in all, M. Lalique is an artist of that type—the creative—which appears most rarely in the course of time. He has given a new direction to the art which he practices, and indicates to those that shall succeed him alluring possibilities of beauty. He has raised the objects which he creates from the rank of toy and talismans up to that of true works of art." The cadre.

What they have done with Astro City has already become the standard to be emulated. Would that the parvenus and arrivistes had even a distant whisper of their abilities.

Imitation may well be the sincerest form of flattery, but it is also the canker on the rose. First comes the voice, then—fainter, smudged and off-key—the echo.

They have elevated toys and talismans to the very high plateau of original art. And I knew them—all but Will—when.

W E STOOD IN A LINE, THE FOUR OF US, there in the West Gallery of the Finlay-Cartier Museum on the Raboy Esplanade, and we stared at a painting on loan from some private collection in the U.K. Or the Netherlands.

It was Sir Lawrence Alma-Tadema's *The Roses of Heliogabalus.*

"Geezus!" Kurt said, softly, all breath and no syllables. "It's as if you're there. It's real. That's all it is... it's palpable."

Let me tell you about that painting. This, from the 1996 comprehensive survey of Alma-Tadema's *oeuvre*, published by the Van Gogh Museum in Amsterdam:

"Marcus Aurelius Antonius became Emperor of Rome at the age of fourteen: his more familiar name, Heliogabalus or Elagabalus, was derived from the Syrian sun god whose worship, along with Eastern court practices, he attempted to introduce to Rome. He was a voluptuary in the style of Nero and ruled Rome amidst venality and debauchery until he was murdered by the Praetorian guard after a reign of only four years (218-222 C.E.)."

Gibbon said Heliogabalus, during his brief reign, was "alike odious and contemptible by all manner of follies and abominations." And Walter Pater called him "an embodiment of pure and unmodified evil."

Brent had the catalogue *raisonné* and, as we stood there in front of the tableau, he read to us:

"Alma-Tadema's young Emperor, dressed in saffron silk, reclines on a couch placed on a raised platform and gazes impassively at the scene below…The guests, lazily reclining on silk cushions, in an arena of pain and pleasure calmly succumb to a sea of petals and their exquisitely decadent deaths."

There was then, as there is now, such a sense of *presence* in that most chilling example of what has come to be known as the Orientalist School of painting, that I cannot express with sufficient vigor how profoundly we four were affected by that viewing, on that afternoon, so long ago.

But both Kurt and Brent—echoed by Alex—said that one day, if the opportunity presented itself, they would strive, undertake, struggle toward…a project that captured *just that* sense of time and place. A project that would encapsulate a superimposed pre-continuum, a fully-formed world.

Astro City.

C HECK OUT ONE OF THE EARLIEST SCENES in this volume. I don't know on which page the panel will fall, but it's the page on which Helia and Thunderhead leave the City and the weather clears. It's the bottom of the three panels. Take a look. That's Central Park West beyond the treetops of Central Park in Manhattan. I used to have dinner with Tony Randall in one of those buildings, and Isaac and Janet Asimov looked out of yet another, next door, directly down on The Tavern on the Green. It's New York, that panel. In Astro?

NOW SH
THE MONS
THE DARK C
PLUS NEWSREE
SHORTS & AIR A
THE MONSTER FROM THE DARK CO

There is a street in Astro City that looks *something* like this view of Central Park West. Not exactly, but close. Brent has filched, what we call in the comics biz "a swipe," and he has plugged it in, because the street he *wanted* to use, the street that *used* to exist in Astro, is now gone, razed to build the elaborate International Merchandise Towers, now the hub of the City's burgeoning clothing industry. So Brent has filched, and we have a simulacrum of the way that corner of Astro City looked oh, fifteen, twenty years ago. Just around the time the four of us studied Heliogabalus's horror show. But, ironically, it is precisely *because* Brent has been compelled to use swipes that I was asked to write the introduction to this most excellent volume of work that exists on a very high plateau.

Turn, if you will, to the fourth page of the Loony Leo story (and, again, I apologize for not being able to direct you by page number). The bottom tier. You see that lovely Brent Anderson rendering of the Ace Theater on Daigh Street? Well, it's New York, again.

But this shot is inordinately special to me.

And it is the impetus for Kurt asking me to preface these fine Astro City stories.

Because I worked directly across the street from the original scene that was snapped as a photo, that Brent swiped to approximate Daigh Street back in the 1950s. (To be exact, in the photo, it's about 1939, and the film playing at the movie house Brent has recast as the Ace was *King Kong*.)

But there was virtually no change on that street between 1939 and 1954 when I worked at the Broadway Book Shop, between the Victoria and Astor Theaters, between 45th and 46th Streets, on Broadway. It's *Broadway*, folks…it's Times Square…and I hadn't yet sold my first story, I had been thrown out of Ohio State University and had

come to New York to make my fortune…and I was working the most fascinating hours anyone could work in that town…seven p.m. till two in the morning. And what a time in my life that was!

I was very poor, I was living in a one-room flat 'way uptown at 611 West 114th Street, off Broadway, across from Columbia University; and every day I would take the IRT subway down to Times Square. First, I'd stop off at the Clam Bar and Flea Circus on 42nd, and say hi to Tiny Tim—yes, the singer who became ultra-famous later with *Tiptoe Through the Tulips* and got married on the Johnny Carson show—but his name wasn't Tiny Tim in those days—but I'm afraid I can't remember what stage-name he was using when he was at the Flea Circus, singing in the basement theater—and then I'd go across 42nd and walk about two doors uptown to the pizza joint where Caruso would give me a terrific slice for 15¢, and add a large papaya juice for another dime. And that was my dinner.

Well, to be precise, it was my *early*, pre-job snack.

Then I'd stroll on uptown to the Broadway Book Shop, and begin selling switchblade knives and the Modern Library editions to tourists and passersby and actors heading to their shows up and down Schubert Alley.

And about ten or ten-thirty, I'd dash between cars on Broadway and the parallel 7th Avenue, and I'd find myself right there in the middle of Brent's swipe, at the Buitoni Spaghetti House, where I could get a swell meal—a plate of *al dente* spaghettini, with one meatball, a chunk of French bread and butter, and an iced tea—for a buck.

Look at that dear panel in the Loony Leo saga. Is it possible that I can convey to you, merest words only, what it meant to me, as I was reading that issue of *Astro City*, and turned the page and found myself staring back through the lens of memory to a scene I hadn't seen in more than forty years? I tell you only this: I am hardly the world's most sentimental soul. No patsy, I. But as I turned that page for the first time, and I let my eyes drift toward the bottom tier, I began to cry. Not hard, not painfully, but my eyes welled, and I was whisked back four decades and more, to my fledgling days as a writer, when I was struggling not only to break into print, to *become* somebody, but to scratch out a living at thirty-five dollars a week, writing all night, sleeping only two or three hours in the early afternoon, hustling my manuscripts to editors in the late afternoon and early evening, and then going off to work my brains out just to pay for that fifteen-dollar-a-week room.

All in that moment. All in that swipe Brent used to recapture the glory of the Ace in the days when Daigh Street was lively and colorful…and not a surrogate Hard Rock Disney Trump Supermall of soulless hotels and tourist crap slop shops.

You see, times change and not all change is

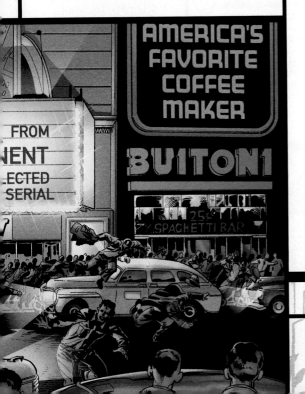

progress. But Brent had to reconstruct the dreamtime of Daigh Street, as this panel reconstructed for me the memory of Times Square in 1954. He *had* to filch and fudge it, to give you the panel correctly. I know he broke his ass trying to find a comparable photo of Daigh and the Ace… but it wasn't to be. So he took a photo of New York in 1939 (unchanged in 1954) and he retouched it. But *that's* why *Astro City* is the uncommon marvel that it is, no matter how many imitators think they can coat-tail themselves into that winner's circle.

It's the touchstone that brings together my tropes of Lalique and Alma-Tadema and the very high plateau upon which *Astro City* sits.

There is a reality to Astro. It is a series of comic book journeys to a *real* place. Realer (yes, improper grammar) than Metropolis or Gotham City or the New York of *Spider-Man*. Realer, perhaps, than many of the places in which you now sit, reading this.

Brent and Kurt and Alex (and now Will, too) go to Astro with regularity. They commute to that real place—as I no longer can, save in reading their work—and they come back with true snapshots of a marvelous land as exotic as Skull Island or Oz or Ultima Thule or Atlantis. They return with stories and anecdotes of ordinary folk like you and me, and the "costumes" who are anything *but* ordinary.

And the *realness* they transcribe is as much sense of place as falling into that sensuous and awful scene in which the depraved Heliogabalus suffocates his courtiers with a *tsunami* of rose petals. As exquisitely rendered in minute detail as René Lalique created his immortal jewelry.

Astro exists.

No minuscule wonder, that.

How difficult it is, as a writer—I tell you absolutely—to create that which *seems* authentic, palpable…*real*. I've been doing it most of my life, and it never grows easier. And Kurt and Brent and Alex and Will do it every issue. They go to the City, and they return with treasures, each one as small and perfect as a Lalique.

I remember my days spent with the cadre in that city of costumes and caring, decades ago, and I dream of the past, and I revel in their presentations of the present. And when Brent has to go back to my past to bring forth a view of Astro that no longer exists, well, it puts me blood and bones and mouth and marrow right in the middle of a work of creativity that exists on a very high plateau indeed.

And that is why I am here. Because I used to spend a buck for dinner at the Buitoni Spaghetti House, when I was young, and the world was filled with costumes and wonder and the awe of standing before a painting that made us all understand that…it's real…geez, it's palpable!

When someone asks you "what is Art?" well, you can hand them this book; and I do not think they will treat you less than nobly for the consideration.

HARLAN ELLISON
Madison, Wisconsin
26 September 1998

Introduction copyright © 1998 by The Kilimanjaro Corporation

HARLAN ELLISON, during a forty-plus-year career, has written 74 books, a dozen or so motion pictures, several dozen teleplays, and more than 1700 stories, essays, articles, columns and commentaries, for which he has won more awards than any other living fantasist. He is the creator of the DREAM CORRIDOR comics from Dark Horse, and a frequent, if controversial, "talking head" on such network tv shows as POLITICALLY INCORRECT and THE LATE LATE SHOW WITH TOM SNYDER. He began reading comic books in 1939.

"Welcome to Astro City"

THEY SAID DON'T BE A *DOPE*, DON'T TRANSFER, NOT *THERE*.

THEY SAID ASTRO CITY'S *CRAWLING* WITH COSTUMES, IT'S TOO DANGEROUS. THINK OF THE GIRLS.

WHK*RANGG*

BUT EVERY BIG CITY'S GOT *SOME* SUPERHEROES -- EVEN IN BOSTON, I SAW THE *SILVERSMITH* A COUPLE TIMES. I SAW THE *BRAHMIN* ONCE, TOO, OUT IN SAUGUS.

AND ANYWAY, I HAD TO *GET AWAY*, GET *CLEAR* -- BEFORE I WALLOWED SO LONG I WOUND UP *DROWNED*.

I HAD TO MAKE A *FRESH START*.

Welcome to

ASTRO CITY

BUT WE HAVEN'T BEEN HERE *TWELVE HOURS*, YET, AND --

JENNY SHELDON HAS A *T-SHIRT* OF HIM.

DADDY, THAT'S *SAMARITAN*. HE'S -- HE'S ONE OF THE GOOD GUYS.

SAMARITAN! MARCY DOERR, KAST!

WHAT DOES THIS *MEAN?* ARE THE *IRON LEGION* ACTIVE AGAIN?

NOT ANY *MORE.*

NOW IF YOU'LL *EXCUSE* ME -- ?

MAN, HE'S RIGHT *THERE*. AND IT'S LIKE THE GROUND'S *STILL* SHAKING. BUT THIS -- IT DOESN'T HAPPEN *ALL* THE TIME.

IT *CAN'T* HAPPEN ALL THE TIME.

TELL ME YOU *GOT* THAT, PETE.

GOT IT.

THEN *LET'S* GO --

-- WE CAN DO MAN-ON-THE-STREET ANYTIME. THIS'LL MAKE THE *NOON REPORT!*

YEAH, UNLESS *SOMETHING ELSE* HAPPENS...

WOW, THAT WAS *COOL!* I'M GONNA *LIKE* IT HERE!

CAN WE SEE MORE, DADDY? CAN WE GO EXPLORING?

WELL, AH --

KAST Channel

DADDY? DADDY, UM... WAS MOMMY *BAD?*

OH, FAITHIE. YOU CAN'T BLAME *MOMMY.* DADDY AND MOMMY WERE BOTH... ...WELL, WE MADE *MISTAKES.* GROWNUPS MAKE MISTAKES SOMETIMES *TOO,* YOU KNOW.

THAT'S RIGHT. PAPER IT *OVER,* MAKE IT OUT TO BE LESS THAN IT *IS.*

THAT'S WHAT YOU WANTED TO *STOP,* ISN'T IT? STOP TEACHING 'EM IT'S OKAY TO LIE, TO HURT, AS LONG AS IT DOESN'T *SHOW?*

MOMMY...MOMMY *LOVES* YOU, YOU KNOW THAT. AND YOU'LL BE SEEING HER AT *THANKS-GIVING...*

HER AND UNCLE *CHUCK,* RIGHT?

OH, *NICE.* QUICK, BEN, SAY SOMETHING POSITIVE ABOUT "UNCLE CHUCK"...

AH...

...HEY, LISTEN TO THAT *WIND!* AND LOOK AT IT OUT THERE --

-- THE WAY THE *DARK CLOUDS* ARE SWIRLING AND THE *WIND'S* RATTLING AT THE WINDOWS.

IT'S LIKE THE WOLF IN *"THREE LITTLE PIGS,"* ISN'T IT? HE'S HOWLING, BUT HE CAN'T GET --

KSSSH

-- AH!

AAH!

WH-WHAT WAS THAT?!

IT'S *OKAY,* KIDS. JUST A BROKEN BRANCH OR SOMETHING -- SOMETHING PICKED UP BY THE *WIND,* AND --

OH.

21

THE *EMERGENCY BEACON* GOES OFF, AND THE LIGHT'S JUST *SWALLOWED* BY THE CLOUDS --

-- NOT THAT IT MAKES A *DIFFERENCE* --

-- BECAUSE THE HEROES ARE ALREADY *COMING* --

-- FLYING UP AT THAT *CREATURE* LIKE THERE'S NOTHING THAT CAN *STOP* THEM --

-- AND I NOTICE SOMETHING I NEVER *THOUGHT* ABOUT BEFORE -- THAT HERE, SEEING THEM IN *PERSON* LIKE THIS --

-- THEY LOOK SO *SMALL* --

I **STAND** THERE FOR I DON'T KNOW **HOW** LONG, TRYING TO SEE WHAT'S HAPPENING --

DADDY? DADDY, THERE'S **RAIN** COMING IN...

THIS IS **SCARY**, DADDY!

-- BEFORE I REALIZE --

THE **TV!** THEY'LL HAVE **NEWS CREWS** OUT, THEY'LL HAVE **EXPERTS** --

-- THEY'LL KNOW MORE THAN **THIS** -- !

MCA X200L TV·Monitor

I FIND THE BOX WE **PACKED** IT IN, AND --

MCA

-- TO TAKE **UNSPECIFIED ACTION** AGAINST THE CITY.

LIVE

PARANORMALISTS AT **FOX-BROOME UNIVERSITY** HAVE IDENTIFIED THE GIANT FIGURE AS A COSMIC ENTITY KNOWN AS **THUNDERHEAD** --

-- THE BEING RESPONSIBLE FOR THE DESTRUCTION OF **DRAKETOWN, ALASKA** LAST YEAR.

KNOWN TO BE OPPOSING HIM ARE THE **FIRST FAMILY**, MEMBERS OF **HONOR GUARD** AND THE **ASTRO CITY IRREGULARS** --

-- PLUS **WINGED VICTORY** AND **THE GENTLEMAN**, MAKING THIS THE LARGEST GATHERING OF SUPER-HEROES IN RECENT MEMORY.

I KNOW YOU'RE TRYING TO DO YOUR *JOB*, BUT IT'S JUST NOT *SAFE* UP HERE TONIGHT.

AND EVEN IF *YOU'RE* WILLING TO TAKE THE RISK --

"-- THERE ARE ALL THOSE PEOPLE *BELOW* FOR YOU TO THINK ABOUT."

"WE'LL -- UH -- HEAD BACK TO *BASE*."

WISE CHOICE. *SEE* YOU.

THAT WAS THE VOICE OF THE *GENTLEMAN* YOU HEARD. THIS HAS BEEN THE *KBAC TRAFFIC COPTER*, ENDING OUR LIVE REPORT...

HEY, CATCH THAT OVER THERE...

HUH?

I DON'T KNOW -- MAYBE IT'S JUST THE *HANGED MAN'S* GOT ME *SPOOKED*, BUT STILL --

"-- WITH SAMARITAN *RUNNIN'* LIKE THAT, WAS THE GENT STEERIN' US AWAY FROM THE FIGHT FOR OUR OWN *GOOD* --

"-- OR BECAUSE THE HEROES ARE *GOIN' DOWN* --"

"-- THE *PEACE* AND *QUIET*."

AFTER AWHILE, THEY RUN OUT OF *STUFF* TO SAY ON TV, AND SITTING INSIDE WITH IT RIGHT OVER OUR *HEADS* IS TOO MUCH.

WE FIND THE *ROOF ACCESS* --

HUH?

HEY, LOOK! EVERYBODY'S *UP HERE* ALREADY!

THERE'S *MRS. DAMIANI,* AND THE GUY WITH THE *DOGS,* AND --

IT'S LIKE A *PARTY* OR SOMETHING -- SOME OF 'EM EVEN BROUGHT UP *LAWN CHAIRS.*

BUT IT'S A *QUIET* PARTY. NO CHATTER, NO CONVERSATION --

-- JUST... *WAITING.* WAITING FOR SOMETHING TO *HAPPEN.*

HI, MRS. DAMIANI! WHERE'S BOBBY?

HIYA, KIDDO. HE'S *DOWNSTAIRS* -- HE'S GOT A PAPER TO WRITE FOR *SCHOOL.*

HE'S WRITING A *PAPER?* WITH ALL *THIS* GOING ON? ISN'T HE --

-- AREN'T YOU *WORRIED?!*

WELL, SURE. BUT WHAT ARE WE SUPPOSED TO *DO?* IT'S OUT OF OUR *HANDS,* YOU KNOW?

AND *HEY* --

AND THEN -- THERE'S A *BOLT*, SO NEAR WE CAN *SMELL* IT --

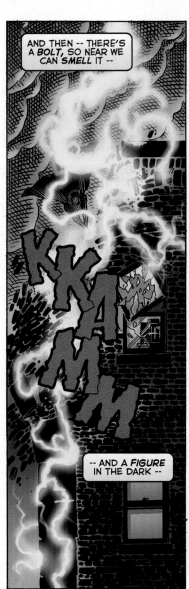

-- AND A *FIGURE* IN THE DARK --

-- AND --

UH -- AH -- AH --

EH?

NO HARM. I PROMISE.

WE ALL DO.

WOW, DADDY! SHE'S *NEAT!* SHE'S ONE OF THE *GOOD GUYS*, RIGHT?

YES, HONEY --

-- YES, SHE IS.

WOW -- PUBLIC WORKS HERE *ALREADY?*

THEY'RE REALLY VERY *GOOD.* I DON'T KNOW WHAT IT'S LIKE ELSEWHERE -- BUT THEY TAKE *PRIDE* IN THEIR WORK HERE.

LISTEN, WE'RE ALL *PITCHING IN* -- -- CLEANING UP *GLASS,* BOARDING UP *BROKEN WINDOWS,* HELPING PEOPLE WHOSE APARTMENTS GOT *DAMAGED.*

WE'RE THROWING A POTLUCK *SPAGHETTI FEED* FOR THE WORKERS, FOR LATER ON. CAN WE COUNT ON YOU FOR A *SALAD,* OR SOME *POP?*

SURE, I -- I'D BE HAPPY TO...

I FEEL LIKE I TRAVELED BACK IN *TIME* --

-- THE WAY EVERYONE'S *HELPING* EACH OTHER -- LIKE THEY'RE ALL IN THIS TOGETHER --

-- IT'S LIKE WHAT *DAD* USED TO TALK ABOUT, ABOUT THE *WAR* --

HEY, DADDY -- THERE'S THAT *TV LADY* AGAIN!

MARCY DOERR, KAST-TV ROVING REPORT, BRINGING YOU THE VIEWS OF THE MAN ON THE STREET.

2

"Everyday Life"

This is where I live.

I live up on the mountain with my **Mom** and **Dad** and **Grandpa** and my **Uncle Nick** and my **Uncle Julie** --

-- 'cept my Uncle Julie's my **great-**uncle, really.

And every **morning**, I get up --

TIME TO GET UP ASTRA!

TIME TO START ANOTHER BRIGHT, SHINY DAY!

-- and do my morning stuff.

HI, 'RANIUM. HAVE A GOOD BREAKFAST.

SHKKKK

"-- BUT THE TWO OF THEM DIDN'T STAY MERELY A *DUO* FOR *LONG!*

"DR. FURST WAS *MARRIED,* AND *DIVORCED,* FOUR TIMES. AND IT WAS HIS *THIRD* WIFE, NADIA, WHO CHANGED HIS LIFE THE MOST --

"-- NADIA, WHO HE FOUND TRAPPED IN A FIELD OF *ALIEN ENERGY* IN *YUGOSLAVIA.*

"HE *RESCUED* HER, FELL IN LOVE, MARRIED HER --

"-- AND WITHIN TWO YEARS, SHE *LEFT* HIM, FOR THE PRINCE OF A *NEAR-LEGENDARY* TRIBE OF *ANIMAL-MEN.*

"BUT THE STORY DIDN'T *END* THERE. IN 1961, SHE WAS *MISSING,* HER NEW HUSBAND WAS *INCARCERATED* --

"-- AND HER TWIN CHILDREN NEEDED *HELP* -- HELP ONLY *AUGUSTUS FURST* COULD PROVIDE.

"HE ADOPTED THEM, AND RAISED THEM AS HIS *OWN* --

"-- AND WHAT WAS ONCE A TEAM OF *TWO* ADVENTURERS BECAME WORLD FAMOUS --

"-- AS THE *FIRST FAMILY!*

"BUT IT DIDN'T END *THERE,* EITHER. IN 1979, DR. FURST'S ADOPTIVE DAUGHTER *NATALIE* SHOCKED THE WORLD --

"-- BY MARRYING *REX,* THE SON OF ONE OF THE FIRST FAMILY'S *GREATEST ENEMIES* --

"-- AND IN 1986, THEIR *DAUGHTER* WAS BORN. THEIR DAUGHTER *ASTRA* --

"-- WHO'S NOW THE MOST *FAMOUS*, MOST *POWERFUL* TEN-YEAR-OLD GIRL IN THE WORLD --

-- AND OUR *GUEST* HERE IN THE STUDIO ON *"ASTRO KIDZ 2-DAY!"*

I'M YOUR *HOST*, STANLEY TRIPP, AND IT'S *GREAT* TO HAVE YOU HERE, ASTRA!

THANKS. IT WAS NICE OF YOU TO *INVITE* ME, MR. TRIPP.

GOTTA ASK -- DID YOUR *MOM* TELL YOU TO SAY THAT?

WELL... YEAH.

THAT'S THE WAY IT *IS* WITH MOMS, HUH? ALWAYS AFTER YOU TO MIND YOUR *MANNERS!*

SO, ASTRA, I'M SURE MOST OF THE KIDS IN OUR AUDIENCE ARE DYING TO *KNOW* --

-- DOES IT FEEL *WEIRD* TO TRAVEL TO OTHER DIMENSIONS AND FIGHT MONSTERS AND STUFF?

UM, NOT REALLY. IT'S *FUN*, BUT...

WHAT ABOUT BEING SO *FAMOUS* -- OR HAVING RELATIVES THAT AREN'T *HUMAN?* THAT'S *GOTTA* BE STRANGE!

I DON'T KNOW...I *GUESS*...

46

REALLY. HEY, I TELL YOU WHAT -- LET'S GO TO THE *PHONES*, AND SEE WHAT THE KIDS OF ASTRO CITY HAVE TO *ASK* YOU.

OKAY?

SURE.

WHAT'S YOUR FAVORITE COLOR?

GREEN.

WHAT GRADE ARE YOU IN?

I DON'T GO TO SCHOOL -- I GET TAUGHT AT *HOME*. BUT I GUESS I'D BE IN *FOURTH* GRADE.

WHAT'S YOUR FAVORITE TV SHOW?

UH, I DON'T GET TO *WATCH* MUCH TV --

DO YOU EVER HAVE, LIKE, *SLUMBER* PARTIES?

NO -- I DON'T REALLY KNOW TOO MANY OTHER *KIDS* --

DO YOU HAVE A BOYFRIEND?

NO, I --

WHAT BANDS DO YOU LIKE? WHO'S YOUR FAVORITE MOVIE STAR?

UH -- I -- UH --

I don't like the questions. There are **too many** of them --

-- and I don't know the right kind of **answers**, and I don't want to be there --

UH-OH. SHE'S *LOSIN'* IT.

MARTY -- SUPERHERO QUESTIONS *ONLY* FROM NOW ON. I KNOW WE WANTED TO PLAY HER LIKE *SUZIE NORMAL*, BUT IT'S NOT FLYING.

NO MORE *KID* QUESTIONS. *NONE*. GOT IT?

YOU'RE TALKIN' TO *ASTRO KIDZ 2-DAY!*

WHAT'S *YOUR* QUESTION FOR ASTRA?

HAVE YOU EVER MET THE IRREGULARS?

OH, *YEAH.* JUICE IS COOL, AN' RUBY'S REAL *NICE.* PALMETTO'S KINDA *ICKY,* THOUGH.

PALMETTO? HE'S THE *COCKROACH* GUY, RIGHT?

HE DOESN'T *LIKE* IT WHEN YOU CALL HIM "COCK-ROACH" --

WHAT'S YOUR UNCLE NICK LIKE? HE'S *YANKIN'!*

OH, UNCLE NICK'S *GREAT...*

-- but it gets better after a while --

-- and after that, the show's even kinda *fun.*

⸽WHEW!⸽

OKAY, OKAY, WE'RE BACK ON *TRACK...*

-- DOES IT FOR *ANOTHER* SHOW, AND WE'D LIKE TO THANK ASTRA FOR SHARING HER *TIME* WITH US --

-- GREAT, REALLY. SHE WAS A TERRIFIC GUEST, AND WE'D LOVE TO HAVE HER BACK --

FSHOOM

DID YOU HAVE A GOOD *TIME*, ASTRA?

I GUESS.

Those **kids** down there -- they know all about T.V. and **boyfriends** and slumber **parties** and bands.

And me -- I know how a T.V. **works** --

-- but I don't even know what **game** they're playing.

MOM?

HOLD ON A SECOND, DEAR. I'M DOCKING *FAMILY-1*...

"-- WE'VE GOT AN INTER-DIMENSIONAL BREAKOUT!

SHOOM

IT'S THE **SILVER BRAIN** -- HE'S FOUND A WAY TO RUPTURE THE BOUNDARIES BETWEEN THE **MENTO-VERSE** AND **HERE** --

-- AND HE'S EMERGED AT THE UNIVERSITY **PSYCH LAB**!

EVERYONE PUT ON THESE **CEREBRA-CIRCUITS**, TO PROTECT YOU FROM HIS MENTAL DOMINATION.

AND **ASTRA** -- YOU'VE BEEN READING THE **FILES**. WHAT CAN YOU **TELL** US ABOUT THE SILVER BRAIN?

UM, HE'S REALLY **SERGEI VLATAROFF**, A SCIENTIST WHO FIGURED OUT HOW TO GO ALL **MENTAL** -- AN' BECAME PURE **BRAIN**.

HE KEEPS TRYIN' TO **ENSLAVE** EVERYONE IN THE WORLD --

-- BUT LAST TIME HE DID, **SAMARITAN** THREW HIM INTO THE **MENTO-VERSE**.

VERY GOOD. ANYTHING **ELSE**?

WELL, HE'S GOT NO **BODY**, SO HE'S ALWAYS GOT TO WORK THROUGH SOME KIND OF **UNDERLINGS**...

AN' **HOLY CATS**, LOOK WHO HE'S USING **THIS** TIME --

–NOW! ASTRA -- MANEUVER EPSILON-SEVEN!

The Gorilla Swarm's a **hive-mind** -- they all share the same thoughts.

So if I disrupt their **transmissions**, they're not **organized** any more --

-- an' they go **berserk!**

GZAA!

OKAY! IN THIS STATE, NATALIE AND I CAN HANDLE THEM -- NO **PROBLEM!** THE REST OF YOU --

UHRZZ!

-- GET INSIDE!

SCHOOL PSYCHOLO

JUST HOW I LIKE TO SPEND MY AFTERNOONS -- -- BEING PAWED AT BY INSECT-HEADED ANTHROPOIDS!

KRASSH

AH, DR. FÜRST AND HIS EXTENDED BROOD!

YOU THINK YOU'RE PROTECTED BY THOSE SILLY *CIRCUITS*, NO DOUBT -- BUT THAT'S ONE OF THE ADVANTAGES OF A *PERFECT MEMORY!*

ALL THAT TIME IN THE MENTO- VERSE, I *REPLAYED* OUR ENCOUNTERS --

-- UNTIL I *DEDUCED* YOUR CIRCUITS' FREQUENCY!

KRAKT

GUS?!

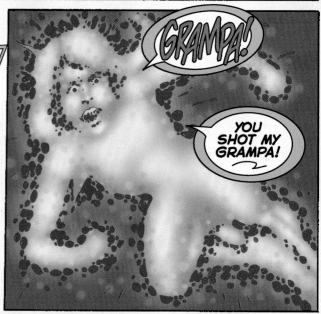

GRAMPA!

YOU *SHOT* MY GRAMPA!

ASTRA, *WAIT!* YOU'VE FORGOTTEN THE BRAIN'S LAST LINE OF *DEFENSE* --

-- THE **ANTI-BODIES!**

ASTRA, YOU CAN'T JUST *BLAST THROUGH THEM* -- THEY'RE ENERGY-BEINGS THEM-SELVES --

-- AND THEY CAN *GRAB HOLD* OF YOU!

Yeah, *duh!*

ZKAK ZKAK

CHOOM

ASTRA!

WE'LL GETCHA BACK, KID!

Uncle Nick an' Uncle Julie are the ones who've forgotten what the Anti-Bodies do.

They grab onto the energy-blasts, just like they do **any** loose energy -- take us all to the power core --

-- and stuff us **in!**

57

I can sense everybody **fighting** outside -- an' it feels like what Uncle Julie calls a **"wild ruckus."**

It seems like it goes on **forever,** but I've got **other** stuff to think about.

Maybe I don't know about **games,** an' I don't know about **sleepovers** and **TV shows** --

-- but I **do** know about energy.

I reach out, an' let myself **dissolve** a little into the energy core --

-- an' I find where the core's powering all of the Silver Brain's **stuff** --

-- an' I shut it all **off.**

HUH?

CLAK TEK

WHAT?!

THE DIMENSIONAL APERSTOMUM -- IT'S BEEN DE-ACTIVATED!

58

C'MON, NICK, REX -- HELP ME GET THIS DINGUS INSIDE --

-- IT'LL MAKE A DANDY ADDITION TO THE TROPHY ROOM!

FINE, FINE. BUT WHEN YOU'RE DONE WITH THAT, JOIN ME IN LAB THREE -- -- WE'VE GOT TO SEAL OFF THE BREACH IN THE MENTO-VERSE -- PERMANENTLY!

UH, MOM?

CAN I ASK YOU A QUESTION?

YOU CAN ASK ME ANYTHING, ANYTIME, HONEY. YOU KNOW THAT. WHAT IS IT?

WELL, IT'S THIS GAME...

SURE. THAT'S CALLED "HOPSCOTCH."

"HOPSCOTCH." WHAT IS IT? HOW'S IT PLAYED?

YOU KNOW, I'M NOT REALLY SURE. I GREW UP WITH YOUR GRAMPA, SO I NEVER PLAYED IT AS A GIRL.

GRAMPA OR UNCLE JULIE MIGHT KNOW, THOUGH. THEY GREW UP AROUND OTHER KIDS, IN ST. PAUL.

GREAT...

...I'LL GO ASK THEM!

NO, WAIT, HONEY --

-- YOU CAN'T ASK THEM NOW!

BUT -- THEY'RE --

I KNOW. THEY'RE HOME. BUT STILL, THEY CAN'T BE DISTURBED. THEY'RE DOING SOMETHING REALLY IMPORTANT.

YOU KNOW HOW IT IS WHEN WE'RE OFF ON AN ADVENTURE, HOW IMPORTANT IT IS THAT WE KEEP THE WORLD SAFE?

DO YOU UNDERSTAND, HONEY?

WELL, THIS IS LIKE THAT, SORT OF. THEY'RE ON A REALLY IMPORTANT ADVENTURE RIGHT NOW, AND THEY'RE NOT BACK YET.

I GUESS...

GOOD GIRL. NOW I'VE GOT TO GO DEBRIEF THE MAYOR'S OFFICE ON WHAT HAPPENED --

-- WILL YOU BE OKAY HERE WITH YOUR ELECTRO-BOOKS AND MISTER SMARTIE?

I GUESS.

GREAT. I'LL BE BACK AS SOON AS I CAN, AND WE'LL MAKE PECAN WAFFLES.

MAGNIFYING

TAP TAP

They know.

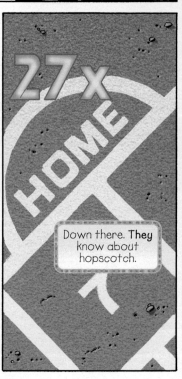

Down there. They know about hopscotch.

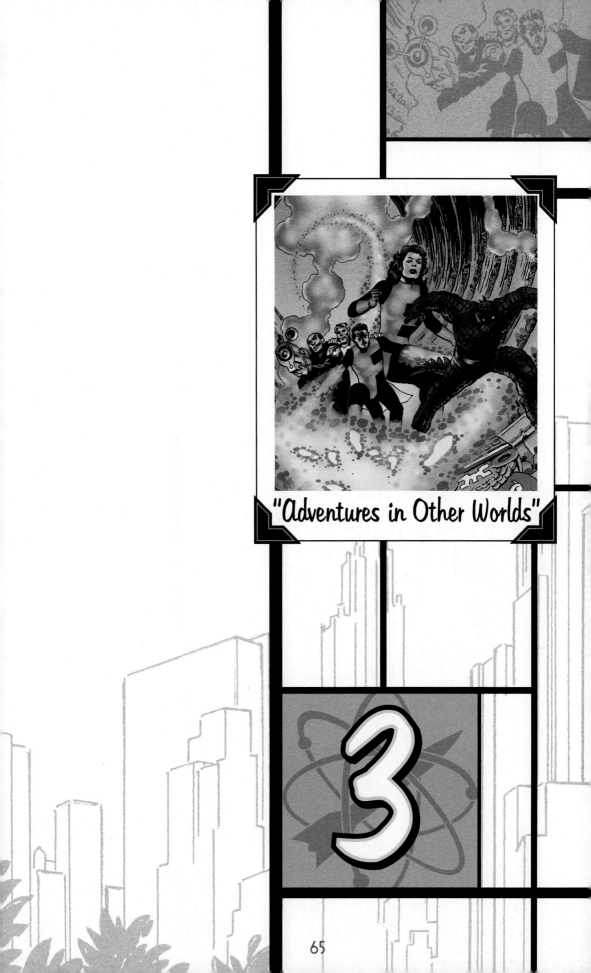

"Adventures in Other Worlds"

3

SIT RIGHT HERE. I'LL HAVE TO TALK TO **MR. LUCEY** ABOUT THIS.

Please Stand Behind White Line

I guess I've got to go to school if I want to learn hopscotch.

Their computers are real old -- like one Grampa gave me when I was four, 'cause he didn't use it any more.

But theirs are way **dumber.**

Please sit Here Until Called

Still, they're **easy** to use -- easier even than shutting off my uniform's **locator chip** --

VERSION 5.1 delux

TREE TREE 5.1 5.1

TAKATAKATAKATA

I'M AFRAID WE DON'T HAVE ANY **RECORD** OF --

-- WHAT ARE YOU **DOING?!**

DON'T TOUCH THAT, CHILD -- THAT'S DELICATE MACHINERY! IF YOU HIT THE WRONG BUTTON --

WAIT, MRS. TOOLE -- I'VE FOUND IT! A TRANSFER FROM OUT OF STATE -- I DON'T KNOW HOW I MISSED IT BEFORE...

THIS IS **ASTRID LJINDERS.** SHE'S A NEW STUDENT HERE, AS OF TODAY --

Astrid Ljinders

"-- AND I'M SURE YOU'LL ALL WANT TO MAKE HER FEEL *WELCOME*."

WHAT DO YOU *MEAN*, MY GRANDDAUGHTER IS *MISSING?!*

NO, AUGUSTUS FURST. *YOU* LOOK.

YOU TOOK *MY CHILDREN* FROM ME, AND RAISED THEM AS YOUR OWN. THAT MAY HAVE BEEN A *GOOD THING*, ALL IN ALL --

-- FOR SURELY, THEY WOULD HAVE HAD A *HARD* LIFE WITH THE *BEAST-PEOPLES*.

NOW LOOK *HERE*, KASPIAN --

BUT THEY ARE STILL *BLOOD* OF MY *BLOOD*, AND TO HAVE THEM TURNED AGAINST ME, AS SO OFTEN YOU HAVE DONE --

-- IS MUCH INDEED TO *ENDURE*.

BUT NOW YOU TELL ME THAT ON *TOP* OF THIS, YOU'RE UNABLE TO SAFEGUARD A SINGLE *TEN-YEAR-OLD GIRL?*

HEY! ENOUGH WITH THE *MOUTH*, ALREADY!

YOU TALK *LOUDLY*, KASPIAN -- BUT WHAT ASSURANCES DO WE HAVE THAT *YOU* HAVEN'T TAKEN MY DAUGHTER?

REX, NO --

YOU... *DARE?*

YOU DARE ACCUSE *KASPIAN* OF THE BEAST-MEN?!

I AM A MAN OF *HONOR*, CREATURE! BAD ENOUGH YOU SULLY *MY DAUGHTER* WITH YOUR TOUCH, BUT TO --

-- NO. ENOUGH. I WILL SEND A MESSAGE THROUGH ALL THE TRIBES OF THE BEAST-MEN. ALL THE WILD WORLD WILL SEARCH FOR HER --

-- AND IF SHE CAN BE *FOUND* BY US, SHE *WILL* BE.

-- TAKE HIS *HEAD* OFF --

CALM *DOWN*, REX -- THIS *MINUTE!*

THANK YOU, KASPIAN. YOU DO US GREAT *SERVICE*, AND WE ARE *INDEBTED* TO YOU.

DO NOT *MISTAKE* ME, AUGUSTUS FURST. I DO NOT ACT IN *FRIENDSHIP*. I SEEK TO PROTECT BLOOD OF MY BLOOD -- -- AND NO *MORE*.

NOW GO --

74

"-- BEFORE I CHOOSE TO REMEMBER THE MANY INSULTS YOU HAVE DONE ME."

UFF!

HAH! YOU *LOSE*, NEW GIRL --

-- AND THERE GOES YOUR *PEBBLE!*

THAT'S WHY I USE A *JACK* INSTEAD OF A ROCK, NEW GIRL.

SEE IT? THAT'S *REAL* GOLD PLATE.

YOU BEAT ME, YOU CAN *HAVE* IT.

BUT NOBODY'S *EVER* BEAT ME -- AND NOBODY'S EVER *GONNA!* I'M THE *BEST* HOPSCOTCH PLAYER AT BOLLING ELEMENTARY SCHOOL --

-- AND *THAT'S* THE WAY IT'S GONNA STAY!

YOU *OKAY*, ASTRID?

I JUST FELL ON SOME GRAVEL -- SKINNED MY KNEE. I DON'T *LIKE* HER.

NOBODY *DOES.* YOU DON'T *HAVE* TO PLAY, YOU KNOW. NOBODY... REALLY *CARES.*

I *CARE.*

If I was home I'd have my **room**. And Mr. Smartie and Mom and Uncle Julie and **everyone**.

But Grampa says you have to endure **hardship** somethimes, when you're on an **adventure**.

And adventures aren't **always** about finding out stuff, he says. They're about **helping** people, too.

And those kids could **use** some help.

And I'm okay. My power and my **programmable uniform** keep me warm --

And I find enough money to buy **food** --

And I practice.

Grampa says practice is **real important**.

YOU LOSE *AGAIN*, NEW GIRL!

READY TO *GIVE UP* YET?

NO. COME ON, LEESHA.

YOU KNOW, YOU LOOK LIKE THAT *ASTRA,* IN THE FIRST FAMILY.

I DO *NOT!* YOU LOOK LIKE A *ROTIFER!*

HUH?

I'M NOT *HER!*

I *KNOW* THAT, SILLY! YOU JUST *LOOK* LIKE HER... SORTA. YOU KNOW, LIKE ON "*SHE'S TWINS,*" ON TV?

UH -- MY MOM DOESN'T LET ME WATCH TV...

YOU'VE NEVER SEEN "*SHE'S TWINS*"? OH, YOU *GOTTA!* YOU WANT TO COME *OVER* TONIGHT? YOU CAN WATCH IT AT OUR PLACE.

REALLY?!

SURE. UM, WHAT'S A *ROTIFER?*

IT'S A MICROSCOPIC ORGANISM. NEVER MIND -- YOU DON'T *REALLY* LOOK LIKE ONE.

WE CAN WATCH TV *TONIGHT,* HUH?

I gotta be careful --

WHOALP!

HEY! YOU TRIPPED ME, MARTRICE!

I DID NOT EITHER!

JUST BECAUSE YOU CAN'T PLAY VERY WELL, THAT'S NO REASON TO BLAME ME!

WHINY LITTLE CRYBABY!

JUST BECAUSE YOU WERE LOSING -- !

I'LL SHOW YOU, MISS MARTRICE -- !

No.

Not that way.

-- SHE DOES *NOT* LOOK LIKE *ASTRA!* NOT EVEN A *LITTLE!*

I THINK SHE *DOES,* MARTRICE.

Everybody's talking about me being **missing.** It was even on TV last night, during "Tooth & Claw."

HAVE YOU SEEN ME?

CALL 1-800-555-FRST
Name: Astra Nadia Furst-Zorus
D.O.B. July 8, 1986 Height 4'8"
Weight: 85 Lbs. Id Marks: None
Hair: Blonde/Straight/Long
Eye Color: Green

LOOK, IF YOU JUST CHANGED HER *HAIR...*

Mom's gonna be **mad.** She's gonna be **real mad.**

But she's always saying how Grampa and Dad and everyone can't be **interrupted** if they're on an adventure.

SHE DOES NOT! SHE'S JUST AN UGLY LITTLE *NOBODY!*

YOU'RE JUST *JEALOUS,* MARTRICE -- 'CAUSE SHE ALMOST BEAT YOU TODAY...

HAVE YOU SEEN ME?

Vitamin D MILK 8oz.

I AM *NOT!*

SEEN ME?

1-800-555-FRST

And I'm on an adventure now...

... so I can't be interrupted either.

SLLLURRRKPP

IT CAN'T BE *INSECTRA* -- SHE'S STILL IN *CUSTODY.*

UGLY MAX IS STILL *CATATONIC.*

WE DON'T EVEN KNOW IF THE *DERELIKT* IS EVEN IN THIS *SPACE-SECTOR,* MUCH LESS ON *EARTH...*

SO MANY *ENEMIES* -- AND IT COULD BE *ANY* OF THEM --

OR EVEN SOMEONE WE'VE *NEVER* FOUGHT, STRIKING AT US JUST BECAUSE OF WHO WE *ARE!*

-- WHERE *IS* SHE, DAD --

"-- WHERE'S MY *LITTLE GIRL?!*"

DONE!

NOT *BAD,* NEW GIRL --

-- NOW STEP BACK. IT'S *MY* TURN AGAIN.

TAK TAK

She starts off like she's not even *looking*. Like she doesn't *need* to.

She *knows* where the jack is. She *knows* where the squares are.

But there's a puddle from the rain last night --

AH!

UFF!

CLANGANGA NGAN

OH, GEE. THERE'S THE *BELL*, NEW GIRL. TIME FOR *SCHOOL*. BUT WE'RE *TIED* -- AND IF YOU QUIT NOW, YOU FORFEIT --

-- AND *I WIN!*

MY NAME'S *NOT* "NEW GIRL" --

THERE YOU ARE, ASTRA!

HI, MOM.

THE *DIAGNOSTI-COMP* SAYS YOU'RE OKAY -- THAT YOUR ENERGY FLUX IS GOOD, EVEN *WITHOUT* YOUR SPECIAL FOODS.

MAYBE WE WON'T HAVE TO *FEED* YOU ANY OF THAT ANY MORE.

BUT ACCORDING TO THE READINGS, YOU MUST HAVE BEEN EATING SOME *AWFUL* STUFF -- !

CORN DOGS, PROB'LY. I *LIKE* CORN DOGS.

OH, HONEY...

WE WERE SO SCARED. THAT'S WHY I YELLED AT YOU BEFORE. WE WERE FRIGHTENED THAT SOMETHING HAD HAPPENED TO YOU --

-- THAT YOU WERE KIDNAPPED, OR HURT -- OR *WORSE.*

YOU UNDERSTAND WHY WHAT YOU DID WAS *WRONG,* DON'T YOU?

UH-HUH.

I SHOULDN'T HAVE GONE WITHOUT *CHECKING* WITH ANYONE, AND I SHOULDN'T HAVE TURNED OFF MY *LOCATOR* CHIP.

I JUST WANTED TO *KNOW.* AND THEN --

I *KNOW,* HONEY.

WE'VE BEEN *TALKING,* THIS AFTERNOON. AND WE'VE ARRANGED FOR YOU TO GO TO SCHOOL AT BOLLING *REGULARLY* --

-- TO BE WITH OTHER KIDS YOUR OWN *AGE,* AND GET TO KNOW WHAT NORMAL LIFE IS LIKE --

-- IF THAT'S WHAT YOU *WANT,* THAT IS...

OH, *MOM!* THAT'D BE *SO* GREAT!

OKAY. YOU CAN START NEXT *WEEK.*

AND WE'LL PROGRAM YOUR COMPUTER TO PICK UP *TV SIGNALS,* SO YOU KNOW WHAT THE OTHER KIDS ARE *TALKING* ABOUT.

BUT NOT *RIGHT AWAY* -- NOT FOR A MONTH. YOU'RE BEING *PUNISHED,* YOUNG LADY -- YOU UNDERSTAND?

I understand.

But still --

"Show 'Em All"

4

Show 'Em All

THE *PSEUDO-GRAVITY INDUCTORS* IN THE SOLDIER'S FEET WORK *SPLENDIDLY.*

THEY WORK SPLENDIDLY IN *ALL* OF THEM.

AND IN A TRICE, THE *AUTOMATIC CAMERAS* AND THE NETWORK OF *ELECTRIC EYES* --

-- ARE MERRILY *TALKING* TO ONE ANOTHER, BUT SEEING *NOTHING.*

THEY ADDED THE ELECTRIC EYES AFTER THE *TECHSPERTS* BROKE IN, TWO YEARS AGO, AND WERE CAUGHT BY *QUARREL.*

THEY PUT *PRESSURE SENSORS* INTO THE FLOOR, TOO. BUT THEY'RE NO *GREAT DIFFICULTY.*

THE JUNKMAN COMES *PREPARED.*

HMM   HMM

IT'S ACTUALLY *FUN.*

Etch – a – Sketch

IT TAKES *HOURS* TO HAUL IT ALL OUT. ONE ELDERLY MAN, WORKING ALONE -- OF *COURSE* IT DOES.

AND MY BACK WILL LET ME *KNOW* ABOUT IT, THE NEXT FEW DAYS.

BUT FINALLY, IT'S *DONE.* FINALLY, THE LAST TRIP IS *BEHIND* ME --

THE ACCESS HATCH IS CLOSED. ALL IS SECURE. THE ACCESS HATCH IS CLOSED. ALL IS SECURE.

-- AND ALL THAT REMAINS IS TO FLOAT IT DOWN TO THE *TRUCK.*

OF **COURSE** NOT, MR. POTTERSTONE. YOU'VE PERFORMED **ADMIRABLY** -- FOR ALL THE **DECADES** YOU'VE BEEN WITH US.

BUT WE HAVE A MANDATORY **RETIREMENT** POLICY HERE AT **EDGECO** -- AND I'M AFRAID WE CAN'T MAKE **EXCEPTIONS**.

B-BUT -- I HAVE MORE **IDEAS**! NEW **INVENTIONS**, NEW **PROCESSES** -- THINGS I'VE BARELY **STARTED** WORKING ON!

IT WAS NO GOOD, THOUGH. I REMEMBERED WHEN **EDGECO** WAS STILL **EDGEFIELD AND WICKERSHAM OFFICE SUPPLIES & REPAIR** --

-- AND THAT WAS APPARENTLY **DANGEROUS** KNOWLEDGE. SO THEY GAVE ME A **GOLD WATCH** --

-- AND A GENTLE BUT **UNYIELDING** SHOVE OUT THE DOOR.

THEY WEREN'T THE **ONLY** ONES, EITHER. **EVERYONE** SAW THE WRINKLES **ON MY** BROW INSTEAD OF THE BRAIN **BEHIND** IT --

I'M **SORRY**, MR. POTTERSTONE. YOUR **RESUME** IS **WONDERFUL**, AND IF YOU WERE ONLY IN YOUR **FORTIES** --

-- YOUR **FIFTIES**, EVEN,

N.R. GISTI

IS THAT **IT**, THEN? IT DOESN'T MATTER WHAT I CAN **DO** -- WHAT I CAN THINK OF, WHAT I CAN **CREATE** --

-- I'M JUST SUDDENLY **OBSOLETE**? OH, LOOK AT THE **CALENDAR** --

-- TIME TO THROW OUT ALL THE **OLD MEN**, LIKE SO MUCH **JUNK**!

THEY'RE **FOOLS**, **ALL** OF THEM! THEY DON'T REALIZE WHAT THEY **HAD** -- WHAT THEY'VE **THROWN AWAY**!

BUT I'LL **SHOW** THEM! HIRAM POTTERSTONE WILL **SHOW** THEM ALL!

THE SUPERHEROES *STOPPED* ME, OF COURSE. PRIMARILY *JACK-IN-THE-BOX* -- HE STYMIED ME AT EVERY TURN.

BUT HE AND THE *OTHERS* WERE JUST HURDLES TO BE *OVERCOME.* I HAD TIME -- TIME AND MY *BRAIN* -- AND THAT'S ALL I *NEEDED.*

AND THIS TIME -- THIS TIME, IT'S *WORKED.* BY THE TIME THEY FINISH CATALOGUING WHAT'S *MISSING* --

-- I'VE GOT THE MONEY LAUNDERED AND TUCKED SAFELY AWAY IN A NUMBERED *GRAND CAYMAN* BANK ACCOUNT.

THEY'RE SCANNING THEIR DATABASES FOR MYTHICAL YOUNG, BRONZED HOLLYWOOD *TECHNO-CRIMINALS* --

-- AND I --

-- I'M STRAIGHTENING MY *SEAT-BACK* FOR THE DESCENT INTO *RIO DE JANEIRO.*

I CAN STILL TASTE THE *CHAMPAGNE* FROM MY COMPLIMENTARY *MIMOSA.*

AND RIO IS EVERYTHING IT *SHOULD* BE.

I STAY IN THE BEST HOTEL -- AND SPEND ENOUGH MONEY TO ATTRACT THE MOST SATISFYING OF COMPANIONS.

I SPEND MY DAYS IN THE SUN --

-- AND MY NIGHTS IN *SYBARITIC LUXURY* --

‹OH, LOOK -- THE *BIRDS OF PARADISE!* IT WAS ON THE RADIO EARLIER --

‹-- HOW THEY CAPTURED *SENHOR TECNICO!*›

‹THEY'RE SO *WONDERFUL* -- SO *VIVACIOUS, SO POWERFUL!* TO FLY LIKE THAT, TO FIGHT FOR *JUSTICE* --

‹-- IT MUST BE THE *GREATEST* THING IN THE *WORLD!*›

‹OH, THEY'RE NOT SO *SPECIAL...*›

-- THEY SHOULD BE JOYOUS, SHOULD BE EXPERIENCES TO BE *EMBRACED* --

-- TO BE REVELED IN AS MY *JUST REWARD* AFTER A *LIFETIME* OF TOIL.

BUT INSTEAD THEY FEEL LIKE -- LIKE *HIDING PLACES.* LIKE REFUGES AGAINST SOMETHING I'M *FLEEING.*

LIKE SHIELDS, LIKE *DISGUISES.* NOT LIKE DESTINATIONS *AT ALL.*

BUT *WHY!* THOSE CAPED, MASKED -- LUNKHEADS! THEY'RE *MORONS! FOOLS!* I OUTWITTED THEM *ALL* --

NOBODY KNOWS A

-- AND *NOBODY KNOWS* A *THING!*

MY TRAVELS *RESUME* WITHIN A FEW DAYS, BUT WITH AN UTTERLY *DIFFERENT* PURPOSE. I KNOW WHAT I NEED TO *DO* NOW.

AND IT STARTS IN *DETROIT.*

THERE'S A BANK THERE THAT SUITS MY *NEEDS* -- A BANK WITH SECURITY SYSTEMS *VERY LIKE* THE BANK IN ASTRO CITY.

BUT *THIS* TIME --

-- THIS TIME, THE GRAVITY INDUCTORS DON'T FUNCTION *QUITE* SO SPLENDIDLY --

-- AND ALL IT TAKES IS THAT ONE *MISTAKE.*

POWERFUL. ATHLETIC. *YOUNG.*

THERE YOU ARE!

HE'S THERE IN UNDER *TEN SECONDS.* *M.P.H.* -- THE ACCELERATION ACE. HERO OF MOTOR CITY.

GLANGLANGLANGLANGLAN

GIVE IT *UP*, JUNKMAN. WHICHEVER WAY YOU *RUN* -- YOU CAN'T ESCAPE ME!

THAT'S A HIGHLY *DEBATABLE* POINT, YOU OVERCONFIDENT *WHIPPERSNAPPER!*

BUT THEN, I CAN OFFER A *COROLLARY:* WHATEVER *YOU* ATTEMPT --

-- YOU CAN'T OUT-*THINK* ME!

Huh? *MARBLES?*

YOU'RE SLOWING *DOWN,* OLD MAN! USED TO BE, I COULD BE *TRIPPED UP* LIKE THAT --

-- BUT I'VE BEEN SIDE-STEPPING MARBLES FOR *YEARS* NOW!

Ah, BUT NOT *THESE,* MY COCKY YOUNG FRIEND --

-- NOT *THESE!*

Wh-*WHAT?*

STATIC ADHESION. SO EASY TO TAKE *ADVANTAGE* OF IT -- TO BOOST ITS EFFECT A HUNDREDFOLD.

STICKING TO ME! GOT TO RUN -- GOT TO *SHAKE THEM OFF!*

BUT THEY DON'T SHAKE OFF THAT *EASILY* -- THEY'RE BUILT *NOT* TO.

AND THEIR NUMBERS *INCREASE* --

-- AND *INCREASE* --

-- AND IN THE END, I DON'T EVEN HAVE TO USE THE *SONIC INVERTER,* TO SHORT OUT HIS *POWER CONTAINMENT HARNESS.*

THERE *IS* A TRICK TO DEFEATING THE *ADHESION MARBLES* -- THERE INVARIABLY *IS.*

WHUMPP

PHYSICAL POWERS, *PHYSICAL* SOLUTIONS.

AND NO DOUBT, HE'LL HAVE FIGURED IT OUT BY THE TIME I HAVE TO USE THEM ON HIM *AGAIN.* BUT NOT *THIS* TIME.

THIS TIME, I GET TO A THIRD OF THE BANK'S AVAILABLE *CASH* BEFORE *CONVENTIONAL* AUTHORITIES ARRIVE.

AND WHILE THEY'RE TRYING TO FIGURE OUT HOW TO GET PAST *MY* SECURITY DEVICES, I TAKE MY *LEAVE* OF THEM.

107

THEY'RE STARTING TO PUT IT *TOGETHER.*

-- DARING TWILIGHT BATTLE BETWEEN THE *BLACK RAPIER* AND THE NOTORIOUS *JUNKMAN* --

THEY'VE REALIZED THE FIRST BANK WAS *MINE* -- AND THEY'RE EVEN STARTING TO FIGURE OUT HOW I *DID* IT.

EXTRA EDITION

Detroit Free Press EXTRA EDITION

JUNKMAN ON CRIME SPREE?

Wary Banks Up Security

'M.O.' in AstroBank Heist is His As Well' S Author

Oldster Eludes Speedster

Astro City Current

The AstroBank Robbery: First Clues Come to Light

• The Man Who Counts the Crime
• America's Most Powerful School
• Elementary School A Report Card
• Restaurant R

I CAN JUST PICTURE YOUNG *YUMIKO* -- YOU *SEE,* SENHOR, THEY WILL *CATCH* HIM NOW...

FOR THAT MATTER, THE MEDIA IS GIVING THE CREDIT TO THE *HEROES* --

-- EXCLUSIVE CAMCORDER FOOTAGE OF THE *NEW ORLEANS STANDOFF,* AND THE *BLACK RAPIER'S HEROIC* --

-- M.P.H. INTERRUPTS BANK ROBBERY, BLACK RAPIER THWARTS SUPERVILLAIN, YADDITA YADDITA *YADDITA.*

WHO'LL STOP THE JUNKMAN'S CRIME SPREE? *THAT'S* THEIR TACK. BUT THEY'LL *LEARN.* THEY'LL *ALL* LEARN.

THAT'S WHAT I'M *DOING* HERE, FIVE MONTHS TO THE DAY FROM WHEN I LEFT. THAT'S WHY I'M BACK IN *ASTRO CITY.*

THE ASTROBANK TOWER LOOKS MUCH THE SAME AS IT DID THE LAST TIME.

A FEW MORE PIGEON DROPPINGS, I'M SURE, SOME MORE WEATHERING -- BUT NOTHING I NOTICE.

I HAVE MUCH THE SAME EQUIPMENT AS LAST TIME. I'M FOLLOWING MUCH THE SAME PLAN.

I EVEN FIND THE SAME ACCESS HATCH. IT'S EASY TO TELL --

-- FROM THE SCRATCHES AND SCRAPES I LEFT GETTING IN BEFORE. AND AFTER DETROIT, AFTER THEY RECONSTRUCTED MY PATH --

-- I'M SURE THEY KNOW IT, TOO.

HEYA, JUNKMAN --

ASTRO

THKASSH

I'LL SAY *THIS* MUCH FOR HIM -- HE'S GOT GOOD *REFLEXES.* IF THE AEROSOL BOMBS HAD *GOTTEN* HIM --

-- THE PAINT WOULD HAVE HARDENED AROUND HIM IN *SECONDS,* STIFFENING AS RIGIDLY AS *STEEL.*

Ah! MY SATCHEL!

BUT AS IT IS, REFLEXES *COUNT.*

WHOA! NICE JETPACK, J.M.!

SHOOM

AS LONG AS I HAD MY SATCHEL, IT WAS MY *BRAIN* AGAINST HIS *BRAWN.* BUT WITHOUT IT, IT'S ENTIRELY A *PHYSICAL* CONTEST --

-- AND AT *THAT* --

ZAK ZAK

MIND IF I TAKE A CLOSER LOOK?!

-- AND AS SPRY AS MY INVENTIONS HAVE *KEPT* ME, OVER THE YEARS --

SLAPP

-- THERE'S REALLY ONLY *ONE* LIKELY OUTCOME.

YOU HAD IT *ALL*, JUNKMAN. YOU HAD *MILLIONS*, FREE AND CLEAR, AND WE DIDN'T EVEN *SUSPECT* YOU.

BUT YOU MADE ONE *MISTAKE* -- YOU CAME *BACK*.

YES...

ONLY AN *IDIOT* WOULD EXPECT THAT SAME PLAN TO WORK *TWICE*. ONLY AN *IDIOT* WOULD *RETURN* LIKE THIS --

AH-AH! WHATEVER YOU'RE *REACHING* FOR -- --THE *ELECTRO-NOSE* IS QUICKER THAN THE --

KZAT

...UNLESS...

UNLESS? UNLESS *WHAT?!*

WITH MY SATCHEL, THEY MANAGE TO FIND MY *HEADQUARTERS*, MY *SUPPLIES* -- EVERYTHING BUT THE *MONEY*.

AND THEY'RE CONFIDENT THEY'LL FIND *THAT*, TOO, THEY SAY.

ASTRO CITY ROCKET
FRI NOV 21 1997
50¢ DAILY

JUNKMAN CAPTURED
Investigators Close to Full Recovery

Criminal's Lair Found in City

IT'S IN ALL THE *PAPERS*, LIKE BEFORE.

IT'S ON *TV*, TOO. BUT THIS TIME, THERE'S A *DIFFERENCE*.

-- NOTED *PSYCHIATRISTS* WILL TELL US *WHY* THE JUNKMAN DID IT -- AND ILLUMINATE HIS *FATAL FLAW* --

THIS TIME, THEY *KNOW* SOMETHING.

THEY DON'T KNOW *EVERYTHING*, OF COURSE -- THEY DON'T KNOW HOW I *MANAGED* IT, FOR INSTANCE.

THE POLICE ARE *WITHHOLDING* THAT, SAVING IT FOR THE TRIAL. AND *JACK-IN-THE-BOX* ISN'T TALKING, EITHER.

BUT THAT'S ALL RIGHT. IT'S COMING.

LADIES AND GENTLEMEN OF THE JURY, THE EVIDENCE YOU ARE ABOUT TO SEE --

-- WILL TAKE YOU *STEP* BY *STEP* THROUGH THE WORKINGS OF A BRILLIANT, BUT *DISTURBED* MIND --

COUNTY COURTHOUSE

-- AND PROVE BEYOND THE *SHADOW OF A DOUBT* THAT THIS MAN -- *THIS MAN* -- SINGLEHANDEDLY COMMITTED THE CRIMES HE'S --

BLAH BLAH *BLAH.* THE PROSECUTOR IS THE *BEST* THEY'VE GOT, THE *TY COBB* OF DISTRICT ATTORNEYS.

MY LAWYER, ON THE OTHER HAND, IS A SCARED LITTLE *KITTEN,* THE INK STILL WET ON HIS CREDENTIALS. NO *COMPETITION.*

SO THE GREAT MAN, THE *GOLDEN ORATOR* -- HE'S GOING TO TELL EVERYONE *EXACTLY* WHAT I DID, AND EXACTLY *HOW.*

AND THEY'RE GOING TO DRINK IN EVERY *WORD,* EVERY *INVENTION,* EVERY EXHIBIT, EVERY STROKE OF *GENIUS.*

AND THEN THE PROSECUTION WILL *REST.* AND I'LL TRIGGER *MY ESCAPE PLAN,* WHICH HAS BEEN IN PLACE FOR *DAYS.*

I'LL *LEAVE* -- AND THEY'LL HAVE THAT MUCH MORE TO TALK ABOUT, *EH?* MEANWHILE, I FEEL THEIR *EYES* ON ME, FASCINATED.

BUT THERE'S NOT MUCH FOR ME TO *DO,* NOT AT THE MOMENT. NOT MUCH, EXCEPT TO *SMILE* FOR THE SKETCH ARTISTS.

IT SHOULD BE A *DELIGHTFUL* SHOW.

YOU ARE NOW LEAVING **ASTRO CITY** PLEASE DRIVE CAREFULLY

5

"Serpent's Teeth"

SERPENT'S TEETH

IN OTHER NEWS, A *CHARITY FUNDRAISER* BANQUET AT THE ROOFGARDEN RESTAURANT WAS *DISRUPTED* TODAY BY THE NOTORIOUS *BRASS MONKEY.*

THE MONKEY ATTEMPTED TO *ROB* BANQUET ATTENDEES, AND WAS ONLY FOILED BY THE INTERVENTION OF *JACK-IN-THE-BOX.*

ACCORDING TO WITNESSES, THE BRASS MONKEY APPEARED TO *OVERPOWER* JACK-IN-THE-BOX --

BLACK-TIE CHARITY CHALLENGE

-- AND EVEN APPARENTLY *HURLED* HIM TO HIS *DEATH.*

BUT THE COSTUMED CRIMEFIGHTER *RETURNED,* AND MANAGED TO FORCE THE BRASS MONKEY TO DROP HIS LOOT AND *FLEE.*

CHARITY GROUPS HAVE BEEN QUICK TO *PRAISE* JACK-IN-THE-BOX'S DECISIVE ACTION IN SAVING THEIR *RECEIPTS.*

I GUESS THAT'S HOW IT *IS* WITH JACK-IN-THE-BOX, *EH*, GORDON? HE ALWAYS *BOUNCES BACK*.

HA-HA! AND I THOUGHT *MY* JOKES WERE BAD, TAMRA.

I'M *GORDON MEADOWS* WITH *TAMRA DIXON*, FOR *KBAC-3*, WISHING YOU THE *BEST* OF EVENINGS.

MADE IT *AGAIN*, ZACK. MADE IT *AGAIN*...

I CATCH THE *NEWSCAST*, LIKE I ALMOST ALWAYS HAVE SINCE SHE GOT MOVED UP TO *EVENINGS*.

AND I CATCH HER RELIEVED *SMILE* AT THE SIGN-OFF, AND CAN'T HELP BUT SMILE BACK, EVEN THOUGH I KNOW SHE CAN'T *SEE* IT.

MADE IT *AGAIN*, TAMRA.

YOU GOING TO GO OVER SCHEMATICS ALL *NIGHT*, Z.J.? THEY'LL STILL BE HERE *TOMORROW*, YOU KNOW --

-- AND THAT PRETTY *WIFE* OF YOURS'LL BE ON HER WAY *HOME* ALREADY...

WHEN YOU'RE *RIGHT*, JACINDA, YOU'RE RIGHT. I THINK I KNOW HOW TO FIX THAT *SHOULDER ASSEMBLY* -- BUT IT'LL WAIT.

I'LL SEE YOU IN THE *MORNING*. YOU AND CRASH HAVE YOURSELF THE *BEST* OF EVENINGS, YOU HEAR?

OH, *YOU.* TAKING THE *SUBWAY?* WE HEAD THE SAME DIRECTION...

NOT TONIGHT, JACE. I'VE GOT SOME ERRANDS TO RUN. *CATCH* YOU NEXT TIME, THOUGH.

I DON'T HAVE ANY *ERRANDS*, OF COURSE. IT'S JUST, WELL --

AND ON I GO, VAULTING, LEAPING, AND THE ROOFS OF *GAINESVILLE* COME INTO VIEW --

-- AND I'M *SMILING* AGAIN, AS BROADLY AS MY *MASK.* I'M A HAPPY MAN, I GUESS --

-- A *HAPPY MAN.*

ONE QUICK CHANGE IN THE ALLEY'S *SHADOWS,* AND...

HOW'S ASTRO CITY'S *HOTTEST* NEWS PERSONALITY?

ZACK!

YOU KNOW FULL WELL I'M LIKE NUMBER *FIVE* OR *SOMETHING.*

OH, I WASN'T *TALKING* ABOUT Q-RATINGS...

WELL THEN.

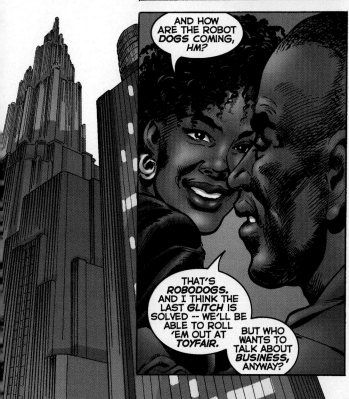

AND HOW ARE THE ROBOT *DOGS* COMING, HM?

THAT'S *ROBODOGS.* AND I THINK THE LAST *GLITCH* IS SOLVED -- WE'LL BE ABLE TO ROLL 'EM OUT AT *TOYFAIR.*

BUT WHO WANTS TO TALK ABOUT *BUSINESS,* ANYWAY?

ZACHARY JOHNSON, I'M HUNGRY AND I'M *TIRED.* AND I RENTED A *VIDEO.*

I'LL RUB YOUR *BACK...*

I GET THERE JUST AS THE MAN *FALLS*, WITH A WET AND *FINAL* GASP.

YOU -- YOU *KILLED* HIM! YOU *VICIOUS* --

AH. THE *TRUE* PERPETRATOR ARRIVES FOR HIS ACCUSATION -- THE *CRIMINAL* WE HAVE TRAVELED THE *DECADES* TO FIND.

TRUE JUSTICE --

GUILTY! GUILTY!

HE STEPS INTO THE LIGHT --

-- CAN FINALLY BE *DONE!*

-- AND MY WORLD TURNS UPSIDE DOWN.

O-OKAY, WHAT *IS* THIS? THE ARM, THE EYE -- *EVERYTHING* -- NO ONE WOULD MISTAKE YOU FOR *ME*.

SO WHO *ARE* YOU?

WHO AM I, ZACHARY JOHNSON? WHO AM I?

I AM THE *BOX!* AND MORE -- I AM YOUR *SON!* YOUR *SON* -- WHOM YOU *FAILED!*

MY -- *SON?*

YOUR SON. YOU DIED BEFORE I WAS BORN, THOUGH. DIED WITHOUT PREPARING ME -- WITHOUT TRAINING ME.

I DIDN'T KNOW THE LEGACY I CARRIED UNTIL I WAS TWELVE. ALL THAT TIME, ALL THOSE YEARS -- LOST!

"BUT I CHOSE TO LIVE UP TO YOUR EXAMPLE NONETHELESS -- TO LIVE UP TO MY HERITAGE!

"I HAD MYSELF CYBERNETICALLY ALTERED, TO AUGMENT MY PHYSICAL ABILITIES, TO GIVE ME THE EDGE I NEEDED."

YOU -- MUTILATED YOURSELF?

I DID! AND I HAVE -- REBUILDING AND IMPROVING MYSELF FURTHER AND FURTHER AS I NEEDED MORE POWER!

I WOULD HAVE DONE ANYTHING TO FOLLOW IN YOUR FOOTSTEPS!

"I MADE MYSELF COLD. I MADE MYSELF HARD, AND BRUTAL -- JUDGE AND JURY IN THE WAR AGAINST CRIME!

"BUT IT WAS NOT ENOUGH! I WAS OVERWHELMED -- CRIME COULD NOT BE STEMMED. AND THEN I REALIZED --

AH-AH, LITTLE *ROBOT-MAN!* LITTLE *MACHINE,* LITTLE *FAILURE!*

I HAVE REACHED THIS ERA -- IN *TIME!* YOU WILL NOT *DEFILE* THE JACK WITH YOUR *TOUCH!*

ANOTHER ONE? I FEEL LIKE I'VE WALKED INTO A MOVIE *LATE* -- A DAVID LYNCH MOVIE, SOMETHING I DON'T WANT TO *SEE* --

IN FACT, FOR EVEN *ATTEMTPING* IT --

AN *ACCOMPLICE!* AIDING AND *ABETTING!*

GUILTY! GUILTY!

BUT WHATEVER'S GOING ON, I CAN AT LEAST *PREVENT* ANY *MORE* LIVES FROM BEING LOST.

-- YOU MUST PAY THE *PRICE!*

NO!

THKASSH

NOBODY DIES!

THKASSH

NOW YOU TWO JUST *STAY* THERE -- AND LEAVE THE CLAWS AND THE CHAINSAWS AND THE GUNS AND THE OTHER WEAPONS *ALONE!*

I WANT TO KNOW WHAT THIS IS ALL ABOUT -- *NOW!*

:MMF MFF:

AHH, FATHER --

129

-- ARE YOU STILL USING THIS PRIMITIVE *MULTI-CHAIN THERMOPLASTIC-RESIN* CONFETTI? IT'S SO EASY TO *MELT*...

HIS *VEINS* -- SOME SORT OF *ACID* --

AND WHAT HE *SAID* --

MY STOMACH *CHURNS*, AND MY THROAT TIGHTENS UP, AND I FIND MYSELF SAYING IT *AGAIN* --

WHO *ARE* YOU?

LIKE *THIS* PATHETIC, CLUMSY CREATURE, SIR, I AM YOUR SON. I AM THE *JACKSON*.

BUT A BETTER, MORE *RESPECTFUL* SON -- AS I AM SURE YOU SEE. FOR *I* DID NOT MATURE IN A *VACUUM*.

"AFTER YOU FELL IN BATTLE, I WAS TAKEN -- BY THE *BROTHERS OF TROUBLE*.

"TAKEN TO THE FAR *FUTURE*, TO ESCAPE THE *WASTING*.

"THERE, I WAS *TRAINED*. THERE, I STUDIED YOUR *LIFE* AND YOUR *WORDS* --

" -- AND *THERE*, AFTER BEING BROUGHT UP IN YOUR LIGHT AND YOUR WAY AND YOUR TRUTH, I WAS *TRANSFORMED* --

"-- *TRANSFORMED* INTO THE *LIVING INSTRUMENT* OF YOUR *WILL!*"

YOU DID THIS -- YOU LET THIS BE DONE *TO* YOU -- AS SOME ATTEMPT TO *HONOR* ME? TO BE *LIKE* ME?

IT HAS TO BE A *TRICK*, I FIND MYSELF THINKING -- AN ILLUSION. IT'S *SMOKE & MIRRORS*, OUT OF JAIL, OR *PROSPERO*, OR -- OR --

HE OPENS HIS MOUTH TO *REPLY*, AND WE HEAR A NOISE --

HM?

HEH-HEH! CONTEMPT! CONTEMPT OF THE BOX!

MAXIMUM PENALTY!

SNIP SNIP

SNIP

THAT HERETIC HAS NO *RIGHT* TO SULLY THIS MOMENT!

I'LL *KILL* HIM --!

I SAID -- NO!

COME AHEAD, THEN -- IF YOU DARE FACE JUSTICE!

THIS ISN'T HOW IT WORKS! IF YOU WANT TO BE LIKE ME, YOU WON'T KILL -- NOT HIM, NOT ANYONE, IF YOU CAN POSSIBLY HELP IT!

EH -- ?

ZZAT

AN ELECTRO-NOSE WILL SUBDUE HIM -- WITHOUT HARMING HIM!

NOW SETTLE DOWN -- I'M NOT THROUGH WITH YOU YET!

YOU -- YOU ARE NOT THE JACK! YOU CANNOT BE!

HOW CAN YOU PREACH AGAINST RIGHTEOUS PUNISHMENT? WAS IT NOT YOU, WHEN THE IRON HORDE ATTACKED WITH LETHAL FORCE --

-- WHO SAID, "OF COURSE, YOU REALIZE, THIS MEANS WAR!"? WAR AGAINST CRIME! WAR AGAINST YOUR ENEMIES!

THE IRON HORDE? THAT HAPPENED, BUT --

THAT WAS BUGS BUNNY! I WAS QUOTING BUGS BUNNY!

AND I WAS MAKING A JOKE, FOR PETE'S SAKE!

I WAIT UNTIL THE *COPS* ARRIVE, THEN WAIT FURTHER, WHILE THEY CALL IN THE *SPECIAL INCARCERATION* SQUAD.

JACKSON *THAWS OUT*, BUT BY THEN THEY'VE GOT HIM IN A JURY-RIGGED *CAGE*.

AND THE WHOLE TIME, NEITHER OF THEM *SAY* ANYTHING. THEY JUST *STARE* AT ME WITH BALEFUL, HATE-FILLED EYES.

MY BOYS. I *BELIEVE* IT NOW -- OR AT LEAST I BELIEVE IT *COULD* BE TRUE. IT SURE *FEELS* REAL.

AND -- IF IT'S A *SCAM* -- WHO WOULD KNOW...

FINALLY, I CAN *GO*. AND I TELL MYSELF I DON'T HAVE TO *THINK* ABOUT IT. I DON'T *HAVE* ANY KIDS. TAMRA AND I *TALKED* ABOUT IT, BUT THAT'S ALL.

ALL I WANT -- *ALL* I WANT --

-- IS *HOME*.

I HEARD ABOUT IT ON THE NEWS -- ABOUT *SOME* OF IT ANYWAY. WHAT *HAPPENED*?

LATER, OKAY? I'LL TELL YOU *LATER*.

THAT *BAD*, HUH? THEN COME *HERE*...

YOU KNOW HOW TO MAKE ME FEEL *BETTER*, TAM. YOU ALWAYS *DO*. SO LET'S TALK ABOUT SOMETHING. *ANYTHING*.

WHAT WAS IT YOU WANTED TO *TELL* ME EARLIER?

WELL, I'D HOPED FOR A *CHEERIER* MOMENT THAN THIS, BUT IT'S GOOD NEWS, SO MAYBE IT'LL *HELP*. ZACHARY JOHNSON...

WE'RE GOING TO HAVE A *BABY*.

ZACK?

ZACK, WHAT IS IT? WHAT'S *WRONG*?

TO BE CONTINUED

ASTRO CITY DEPT. OF PUBLIC WORKS

142

6

"Father's Day"

Father's Day

"MY FATHER WAS THE *ORIGINAL* JACK-IN-THE-BOX."

"HE WAS A DESIGNER FOR *WHAMCO TOYS.* A BLACK DESIGNER IN THE EARLY SIXTIES WAS *UNUSUAL,* BUT HE WAS TALENTED --

"-- SO THEY *HIRED* HIM, AND PAID HIM HALF WHAT LESS PRODUCTVE *WHITE* DESIGNERS MADE.

"BUT THEN, BY *CHANCE,* HE DISCOVERED THAT SOME OF HIS TOY DESIGNS WERE BEING USED IN *WEAPONS* --

"-- WEAPONS USED BY THE *UNDERWORLD.*

"HE TRIED TO GET TO THE BOTTOM OF IT AT *WHAMCO,* BUT ALL THAT HAPPENED WAS THAT HE GOT *FIRED.*

"STILL, HE *DIDN'T* LET IT GO. HE TRIED TO FIND THE *LINK* BETWEEN WHAMCO AND THE MOBS -- TRIED TO *EXPOSE* IT.

"NOBODY *BELIEVED* HIM, BUT WHAMCO WANTED HIM TO *SHUT UP* ANYWAY.

"SO THEY HAD HIS FATHER -- MY *GRANDFATHER* -- KIDNAPPED.

"THAT'S WHEN HE CUSTOMIZED SOME OF HIS *TOY DESIGNS,* WORKED UP A COSTUME --

"-- AND BECAME *JACK-IN-THE-BOX* -- FIRST TO RESCUE MY GRANDFATHER, AND THEN TO CONTINUE HIS *INVESTIGATION.*

"HE TOOK ON THE *MOBS,* HE TOOK ON *WHAMCO,* AND EVENTUALLY HE EXPOSED THEM. HE *WON.*

"BUT HE STILL KEPT *FIGHTING* -- FOR OTHERS WHO'D BEEN VICTIMIZED, WHO NEEDED *HELP.* HE'D BECOME A *HERO.*

"AND THEN ON *OCTOBER 13, 1983* --

"-- HE *DIED,* KILLED IN AN EXPLOSION WHILE FIGHTING MINIONS OF THE *UNDERLORD.*

"BUT HE TOOK THE *UNDERLORD* DOWN, TOO -- OR SO IT SEEMED. HE DIED *SAVING* PEOPLE. MAKING THE WORLD A *BETTER PLACE.*

"ME, I WAS TWELVE. AND I DIDN'T KNOW *ANY* OF THIS.

"BUT I FOLLOWED IN MY FATHER'S *FOOTSTEPS* -- STUDYING *ENGINEERING,* DESIGNING TOYS OF MY *OWN* --

"-- AND WHEN I WAS EIGHTEEN, MY *MOTHER* DIED TOO. AND IN THE PROCESS OF SETTLING THE ESTATE --

"-- I FOUND MY FATHER'S *GADGETS* AND *JOURNALS.* I FOUND THE *TRUTH.*

"THERE WAS A *LOT* IN THOSE JOURNALS -- *INCLUDING* THE UNDERLORD'S TRUE IDENTITY. AND HE *WASN'T* DEAD.

"MY MOTHER EITHER NEVER *KNEW,* OR SHE THOUGHT I WAS TOO YOUNG TO KNOW. SO I DIDN'T GET *TOLD.*

"I BECAME THE *SECOND* JACK-IN-THE-BOX THEN. TO BRING IN THE UNDERLORD, TO GET *JUSTICE* FOR MY FATHER.

Veidt St.

"AND BY THE TIME I *MANAGED* THAT --

"-- I STAYED IN COSTUME, LIKE *HE* HAD. I BECAME A SUPERHERO, TOO.

YOU *KNOW* ALL THAT. I'VE TOLD IT A DOZEN TIMES. BUT THERE'S MORE *TO* IT. THERE'S A PART I'VE NEVER REALLY *TALKED* ABOUT.

THAT'S THE PART ABOUT WHAT IT'S LIKE TO BE TWELVE YEARS OLD AND HAVE YOUR FATHER JUST... *VANISH.*

"I DIDN'T KNOW WHAT HAD *HAPPENED.* MY MOM SAID HE WAS DEAD, BUT THERE WAS NO BODY, NO *FUNERAL.*

"WAS HE *REALLY* DEAD? OR WAS HE JUST *GONE?* DID HE LEAVE -- DID HE JUST NOT *LOVE* US? I DIDN'T KNOW.

"I CAME UP WITH ALL KINDS OF FANTASIES -- HE WAS A *SPY,* OR AN *UNDERCOVER COP.* OR IN THE *WITNESS PROTECTION PROGRAM.*

"SOMETIMES, I EVEN IMAGINED HE WAS A DARING *CRIMINAL MASTERMIND,* ON THE RUN FROM THE LAW. *STUPID,* HUH?

"BUT THE BOTTOM LINE WAS, HE WAS *GONE.* AND I SPENT SIX YEARS TRYING TO *FILL* THAT HOLE --

"-- TRYING TO WIN THE APPROVAL OF A *GHOST,* TO BE WHAT MY FATHER WOULD HAVE WANTED WITHOUT KNOWING WHAT THAT *WAS.*

"AND IN THE END, WHEN I LEARNED THAT THE TRUTH EXCEEDED *ALL MY FANTASIES,* I WAS *PROUD,* AND I WAS HONORED --

"-- BUT STILL, THERE WAS A PART OF ME THAT FELT *HOLLOW* --

"-- THAT FELT LIKE MY FATHER HAD CARED MORE ABOUT *FIGHTING CRIME* THAN ABOUT HIS *FAMILY.*"

SO NOW, WHEN YOU TELL ME YOU'RE *PREGNANT* -- AND *I'M* THE ONE GOING OUT THERE EVERY NIGHT --

I -- I THOUGHT YOU *WANTED* KIDS. I THOUGHT YOU *WANTED* THIS!

I DO, TAMRA, I *DO.* IT'S JUST --

-- I DIDN'T THINK WE'D BE HAVING KIDS THIS *SOON.* I DIDN'T THINK ABOUT WHAT IT *MEANT* --

"AND AFTER WHAT HAPPENED *TONIGHT,* WITH THOSE -- THOSE TWISTED VERSIONS OF WHAT OUR CHILD COULD *BECOME* --

"-- IT'S MADE ME THINK ABOUT WHAT COULD *HAPPEN,* AND WHAT THAT COULD MEAN TO A *BABY.*

I NEVER *MINDED* RISKING MY LIFE -- IT'S SOMETHING I DO *WILLINGLY,* AND SOMETHING YOU *KNEW* I DID WHEN YOU MARRIED ME.

BUT A BABY -- WE CAN'T EXACTLY *ASK* HIM -- OR HER -- IF IT'S OKAY, CAN WE? IF HE'D MIND GROWING UP WITHOUT A *FATHER?*

I CAN RISK *MY* LIFE. BUT CAN I RISK THE LIFE OF MY CHILD'S *FATHER?* IS THAT FAIR TO *HIM?*

OR *HER.*

I'VE NEVER *ASKED* YOU FOR THIS -- EVEN THOUGH I KNEW WHAT IT COULD MEAN -- BUT, WELL, YOU COULD *QUIT...*

HOW? CAN I READ IN THE PAPER ABOUT MURDER -- ABOUT *RAPE,* AND MORE -- AND KNOW I COULD HAVE *STOPPED* IT?

HOW COULD I *LIVE* WITH MYSELF?

I CAN'T BELIEVE I'M *SAYING* THIS -- CAN'T EVEN BELIEVE WE'RE TALKING ABOUT YOU *DYING* --

-- BUT FIREMEN, COPS, SOLDIERS -- *THEY* RISK THEIR LIVES, AND *THEY* HAVE FAMILIES...

I *KNOW.*

MAYBE IT'S JUST *ME.* MAYBE IT'S HOW I *GREW UP.* BUT I KNOW -- I KNOW WHAT I COULD BE PUTTING THAT BABY *THROUGH* --

-- AND I DON'T KNOW IF I CAN *DO* THAT.

SO WHAT YOU'RE SAYING -- YOU'RE SAYING YOU DON'T WANT TO *HAVE* THIS BABY?

I DIDN'T SAY THAT. I DIDN'T *SAY* THAT. I JUST --

"-- JUST NEED TO *THINK,* THAT'S ALL."

DAMMIT, THIS WAS SUPPOSED TO BE A *HAPPY* NIGHT.

THIS WAS SUPPOSED TO BE *GOOD* NEWS...

DETECTIVE WILLIAMS LETS ME IN, TO WHERE THEY'RE BEING HELD FOR *PROCESSING*, BEFORE THEY'RE MOVED TO *BIRO ISLAND*.

I *LOOK* AT THEM, AND I DON'T *KNOW* WHAT TO THINK.

ARE THEY MY SONS -- SOMETHING THAT MY CHILDREN COULD *BECOME*, IN SOME WARPED FUTURE?

COULD THIS REALLY *HAPPEN?* IF I DIED, COULD THE CHILD GROWING INSIDE TAMRA *BECOME* -- SOMETHING LIKE *THAT?*

IS THAT REALLY ALL I'VE GOT TO *GIVE* TO MY FAMILY -- PAIN, AND A TWISTED, HARMFUL *LEGACY?*

IS IT?

YOU MUST BE JUDGED, FATHER. JUDGED FOR FAILING YOUR SON. FOR FAILING YOUR WORLD.

YOU ARE A *HERETIC* AND A *FALSE PROPHET*, BLIND TO YOUR OWN TEACHINGS. YOU WILL BE *CLEANSED.*

151

WE HAVE AGREED, FATHER. WE WILL NOT TELL THE *PATHETIC POLICE* OF THIS ERA ANYTHING *ABOUT* YOU. KEEP YOUR SECRETS --

UNTIL THE DAY WE *PUNISH* YOU. WE SHALL BE FREE -- AND WE SHALL BE THE *INSTRUMENT* OF YOUR *DESTRUCTION.*

I'M STILL TAKING THAT IN -- STILL REALIZING THAT THEY COULD HAVE JUST *ANNOUNCED* MY *TRUE IDENTITY* --

-- WHEN --

FAREWELL, FATHER --

...WE'LL BE *BACK...*

WH- *WHAT* -- ?

LANGLANGLANGLANGLANGLANG

THEY'RE -- THEY'RE *GONE!*

AFTER THAT, THERE'S NOT MUCH TIME TO *THINK* -- NOT FOR A WHILE.

THE COPS DON'T REALLY THINK I HELPED THEM *ESCAPE,* BUT THEY'VE GOT TO CHECK IT OUT -- MAKE SURE.

BUT EVENTUALLY, THEIR TECHS TELL THEM THE SHACKLES WEREN'T *TAMPERED* WITH -- THE CELL DOORS WEREN'T EVEN *OPENED.*

152

-- SO IF YOU *ENCOUNTER* THEM AGAIN, OR HEAR ANYTHING --

OF *COURSE*, DETECTIVE, I'LL LET YOU --

-- HEY!

SOMEONE YOU *KNOW*, JACK?

THAT'S ROSCOE JAMES -- ONE OF THE *TROUBLE BOYS*.

HE'S A GOOD KID -- A LITTLE *RAMBUNCTIONS*, MAYBE, AND A *SMART-MOUTH*. BUT HE'S NO CRIMINAL.

WHAT'S HE BEING *BROUGHT IN* FOR?

TURNS OUT IT'S *ASSAULT*, AND *ROBBERY*.

SOMEONE HAD *BEATEN* A WOMAN, TAKEN HER PURSE AND A WATCH -- AND THE DESCRIPTION SHE GAVE FIT *ROSCOE*.

THE *TIMING'S* WRONG. YOU SAY THE ASSAULT HAPPENED AROUND *TEN* --

-- BUT THAT'S WHEN I FINISHED FIGHTING THOSE TWO WHO WERE *UPSTAIRS*, AT THE WRECKING YARD. AND ROSCOE WAS *THERE*.

YOU *SURE* ABOUT THAT?

BUT IT *COULDN'T* HAVE BEEN HIM.

THEY *LISTEN* TO ME, AND IN A WHILE...

SUPPOSE YOU WANT ME TO *THANK* YOU, JACKS. THAT WHAT YOU WAITIN' *AROUND* FOR?

NO -- I JUST WANTED TO MAKE SURE YOU WERE *OKAY*.

154

-- AND EVERY TIME THERE'S *TROUBLE*, AND I FEEL I HAVE TO GO --

-- HOSTAGE SITUATION AT THE ROBINSON HOTEL --

-- WE *BOTH* WONDER IF THIS IS THE TIME I WON'T BE COMING *BACK*...

AND THEN ONE DAY, AS I'M TRYING TO SOLVE AN *ENGINEERING PROBLEM*, GOING BACK TO FIRST ASSUMPTIONS AND *RETHINKING* --

-- I GET AN *IDEA* --

ZACK! ZACK, YOU *HOME?*

I WAS GOING TO MAKE THAT *ZUCCHINI CHICKEN* FOR DINNER, IF THAT'S OKAY WITH --

CLK

-- JACK-IN-THE-BOX, IN COMBAT WITH THE *BRASS MONKEY* AND HIS GORILLA TROOPS, AT THE VEIDT STREET ART GALLERY.

OUR CAMERAS WERE THERE FOR THE OPENING, AND SO WE'RE ABLE TO BRING YOU THIS DRAMATIC, *LIVE* FOOTAGE --

NEVER MIND.

ALL OF A SUDDEN, I'M NOT *HUNGRY*...

NG-AAHH! YEAH, YEAH! I KNOW!

UNGH

THE HANDSPRINGS -- I'M USIN' 'EM, SEE?

WRAK

AN' THE CONFETTI, TOO!

I JUST FORGOT FOR A SEC, THAT'S ALL!

TH'KASSH

AND THEN --

WH -- ?

WHAT'S THAT NOISE?

IS -- IS SOMEBODY HERE?

SHOW YOURSELF!

ZACK ?!?

BEHIND YOU, *BEHIND* YOU! KEEP *MOVING* -- DON'T LET THEM GET A *BEAD* ON YOU!

USE YOUR *WEAPONS*, REMEMBER YOUR *TRAINING*, USE THE *ADVANTAGE* THEY GIVE YOU! THERE'S ONLY TWO LEFT --

YEAH, YEAH --

-- AN' NOW THERE'S ONLY ONE!

AN' IN A *MINUTE* --

-- WE CAN DROP THAT TO *ZERO!*

ZACK -- WHAT'S GOING ON? YOU SAID A WHILE AGO YOU'D HAD AN *IDEA,* BUT --

-- WHO *IS* THAT OUT THERE?

162

OWWWWW!

CHUMP.

DON'T THINK OF HIM AS WEAK, JUST BECAUSE HE'S SMALL!

THE MONKEY WAS ORIGINALLY A JANITOR AT A LAB DOING RESEARCH INTO MENTAL TRANSFERENCE --

-- HE USED THEIR MACHINES TO PROJECT HIS MIND INTO A BRASS MONKEY STATUE, PLANNING TO USE IT FOR BURGLARIES --

-- BUT WHILE HE WAS STILL IN THE STATUE, HIS REAL BODY GOT KILLED.

HE'S SOLID BRASS! HE'S INHUMANLY STRONG --

-- BUT HE'S GOT A HUMAN MIND! YOU CAN'T FORGET THAT!

YEAH, YEAH -- YOU TOLD ME, ALREADY!

SHRRRIPPPP!

YOU OKAY, JACK-IN-THE-BOX? YOU FEELIN' ALL RIGHT?

MUTTERIN' TO YOURSELF, MAKIN' STUPID MISTAKES, LIKE THINKIN' YOUR CONFETTI CAN HOLD ME --

-- I'D HATE TO THINK I'D KILLED YOU WHILE YOU HAD A COLD OR SOMETHIN'!

NOT THAT IT'S GONNA STOP ME, MIND YOU...

USE THE FOOTAPULTS, ROSCOE -- STAY *AWAY* FROM HIM!

DON'T LET HIM *GRAPPLE* WITH YOU -- HE'S TOO *STRONG!*

ARE YOU SURE IT'S OKAY TO *RECRUIT* HIM? THE RISK --

IT'S A *RISK*, YEAH. BUT AT LEAST *HE* CAN ACCEPT IT *CONSCIOUSLY* --

-- AND IT'S NOT LIKE THE STREETS OF BAKERVILLE ARE A WALK IN THE *PARK.* BELIEVE ME, HE *KNEW* WHAT HE WAS AGREEING TO.

HE NEEDS A WAY *OUT* -- AND THIS WAY, I CAN GIVE HIM SOME MONEY FOR SCHOOL, FOR *COLLEGE* --

-- AND HE'LL *TAKE* IT. HE WOULDN'T HAVE TAKEN *CHARITY.*

TSSH

OOP -- I HOPE THE GALLERY'S *INSURED* -- !

GET HIM *OUTSIDE*, ROSCOE -- HE'S USING THE CLOSE QUARTERS *AGAINST* YOU! JUST GET HIM OUT, AND CHASE HIM OFF!

HE'S NOT A THREAT TO *INNOCENTS* -- HE'S JUST A THIEF! CHASE HIM OFF -- WE'LL CATCH UP TO HIM SOME OTHER TIME!

AND I'M THINKING HOW *NONE* OF 'EM -- NONE OF MY *"BOYS"* -- SAID ANYTHING LIKE *THIS.*

MAYBE THIS IS THE *CHANGE* WE NEEDED. MAYBE THE BABY HAS A *CHANCE* NOW. AND ROSCOE --

EEEOOOEEEOOOEEEOOOEE

COPS! I BETTER --

DON'T *WORRY* ABOUT IT, ROSCOE --

-- THEY'RE HERE FOR THE *BRASS MONKEY,* NOT YOU. YOU'RE THE *HERO,* REMEMBER?

AND YOU DID *GOOD. REAL GOOD.*

HUH.

YEAH, I GUESS I *DID,* DIDN'T I?

SO WHEN DO WE GO AFTER THE *DEACON,* HUH?

NOT RIGHT *AWAY,* ROSCOE. BUT WE'LL DO IT -- IN *TIME.*

I'VE GOT TO ADMIT, I HAD MY *DOUBTS.* HE TOOK TO THE TRAINING LIKE HE'D BEEN *WAITING* FOR IT ALL HIS LIFE. BUT STILL --

-- THERE'S A DIFFERENCE BETWEEN AN EXERCISE AND *REAL BULLETS.*

BUT HE DID JUST *FINE.* NOT WHAT *I'D* HAVE DONE, MAYBE, BUT FINE NONETHELESS. I BREATHE A SIGH OF *RELIEF* --

-- AND SEND THE *'RETURN'* COMMAND TO THE DOODLEBUG.

AND TAMRA GETS THIS *LOOK* IN HER EYE...

YOU REALIZE YOU JUST TOOK ON AN *ADOPTIVE SON* -- EVEN BEFORE THE *REAL* ONE'S HERE.

IF THAT'S WHAT IT *TAKES,* HONEY.

AND ROSCOE'S A *GOOD KID* -- HE DESERVES A CHANCE. THIS IS KIND OF AN *EXTREME* CHANCE, TRUE, BUT --

IT'S GOING TO BE A LOT OF *WORK.* YOU SURE IT'S THE RIGHT *THING*?

NO, I'M *NOT.*

FOR ALL I KNOW, THIS COULD BE THE *EXACT* STEP THAT'LL CREATE ONE OF THOSE FUTURES -- OR SOMETHING *WORSE.*

BUT IT'S THE BEST I CAN *THINK* OF. AND IN THE END --

-- ISN'T THAT HOW IT WORKS FOR *ANY* PARENT?

HAVE I TOLD YOU RECENTLY HOW MUCH I *LOVE* YOU?

SEEMS TO ME I'VE *HEARD* IT A TIME OR TWO, YEAH. BUT I'M NOT *TIRED* OF IT. C'MERE.

YOU ARE NOW LEAVING **ASTRO CITY** PLEASE DRIVE CAREFULLY

"In the Spotlight"

7

JOSS RYERSON Account Exec

Paul ARTHUR
ADVERTISING

AstroBank Tower
Suite 1300
Astro City

WELL -- I MEAN -- IT'S ONLY SIX COMMERCIAL SPOTS FOR A LOCAL *TOYOTA* AGENCY --

-- OR JUST *FOUR,* IF YOU'D RATHER --

-- AND, I KNOW THE *MONEY'S* NOT GREAT -- BUT WE COULD MAYBE GET THE CLIENT TO PONY UP SOME *MORE* --

Pfah! IT'S THE "*ENTERTAINMENT INDUSTRY!*" TELEVISION, MOVIES, ADVERTISING -- ALL THE *SAME!*

AND YOU WANT ME TO JUST JUMP BACK *IN,* AS IF NOTHING'S *HAPPENED.* JUST WIPE MY WHOLE *LIFE* AWAY, IS THAT IT?

WELL, ah --

-- I *DON'T* --

Ah, I SEE. YOU'RE *YOUNG.* YOU DON'T *KNOW* ANY OF IT -- THAT'S PROBABLY WHY THEY *SENT* YOU.

WELL, GRAB A CUP OF COFFEE FROM THE URN OVER THERE --

-- AND I'LL TELL YOU A *STORY...*

"IT WAS *1946.*

"THE WAR WAS *OVER,* ROMEYN FALLS WAS *REBUILDING* -- AND THEY WERE ALREADY TALKING ABOUT THE *NAME-CHANGE* --

"-- THOUGH THE MEASURE HADN'T *PASSED* YET.

"IT WAS A LATE NIGHT AT THE *ACE THEATER,* ON *DAIGH STREET,* AND JUST LIKE AT *OTHER* THEATERS ACROSS TOWN --"

NOW SHOWING

THE **MONSTER** FROM THE **DARK CONTINENT**

PLUS NEWSREELS - SELECTED SHORTS - & AIR ACE THE SERIAL

THE **MONSTER** FROM THE **DARK CONTINENT**

AMERICA FAVORIT COFFE

SPAGHETTI BAR

"-- AND OUT IN THE LOBBY --"

Hm?

"I'D NEVER EXISTED BEFORE, NOT REALLY. AND IT WAS BEWILDERING.

HOW... ODD!

"I DIDN'T KNOW WHY ANYTHING WAS HAPPENING --

"-- OR WHY THEY WERE SCREAMING AT ME."

EEEEE!

ANOTHER ONE!

THEY'LL KILL US! THEY'LL KILL US ALL!

RUN! RUN!

COMING SOON

PLEASE -- I DON'T --

"ALL IN ALL, IT WAS A PRETTY CONFUSING SCENE TO COME IN ON."

KSMASSS!

KRARRR

OH, NO YOU DON'T!

"BUT IT WAS FASCINATING, TOO.

"I WATCHED, TRYING TO FIGURE OUT WHAT WAS GOING ON --

"IT WAS THE GENTLEMAN WHO *RESCUED* ME. HE REALIZED WHAT MUST HAVE *HAPPENED* --"

I FEEL SO -- SO STRANGE --

PEOPLE! PEOPLE, *LISTEN* TO ME!

THIS MAN, THIS -- WELL, THIS *LION* -- JUST *SAVED YOU ALL!* AND HE WOULDN'T HAVE BEEN HERE TO *DO* IT -- WOULDN'T HAVE BEEN HERE AT *ALL* --

-- IF PROFESSOR *BORZOI'S* *BELIEF RAY* HADN'T BROUGHT HIM TO LIFE, USING *YOUR* BELIEF IN HIM!

AND NOW HE'S *DYING!* HE SACRIFICED THE THING THAT BROUGHT HIM TO LIFE -- TO SAVE *YOU!* BUT YOU CAN SAVE *HIM,* IN TURN --

-- IF YOU'LL ONLY *BELIEVE!*

BELIEVE IN HIM! BELIEVE HE'S *REAL!* IT'S THE ONLY THING THAT'LL *SAVE* HIM!

"IT WAS A GOOD IMPULSE. A *GENEROUS* IMPULSE. BUT THE GENTLEMAN'S *ALWAYS* BEEN LIKE THAT.

"HE DIDN'T THINK IT THROUGH. HE JUST *ACTED* -- JUST STIRRED THE CROWD INTO *BELIEVING* IN ME --"

WH- *WHAT...?*

"-- AND THAT'S HOW ALL MY TROUBLES *BEGAN.*

"FIRST THERE WAS THE *COURT CASE*. I'D STUCK AROUND -- HAD A FEW *ADVENTURES* WITH THE GENTLEMAN --

"-- GOTTEN IN THE *NEWS* A LITTLE --

"-- WHEN I HEARD FROM THE STUDIO'S *LAWYERS*, CLAIMING THAT THEY'D MADE ME UP -- SO I WAS THEIR *PROPERTY*.

"WELL, THEY SHOULD HAVE MADE UP SOMEONE MORE *TRACTABLE*. I DIDN'T *LIKE* IT, AND NEITHER DID THE GENT --

"-- SO HE FOUND ME A *LAWYER*, AND WE WERE GOING TO FIGHT IT. WE'D PROBABLY HAVE *LOST* --

"-- THIS WAS THE *FORTIES*, AND ARTIFICIAL BEINGS WEREN'T *AROUND* MUCH, NOT LIKE NOW --

"-- BUT I HAD A REPUTATION AS A *POCKET HERO*, YOU KNOW -- AND THE STUDIOS DIDN'T WANT THE BAD *PUBLICITY* --

"-- THEY DIDN'T WANT TO SEEM LIKE *BAD* GUYS, ENSLAVING A PUBLIC CELEBRITY WHO'D SAVED *LIVES*.

"SO WE *SETTLED* OUT OF COURT.

"THEY OFFERED ME A *DEAL* -- THEY'D GET THE RIGHTS TO *MY EXISTING* CARTOONS IN PERPETUITY --

AGREEMENT

"-- BUT THEY'D HAVE NO CLAIM ON *ME*. AND THEY EVEN OFFERED ME A *CONTRACT*, FOR FEATURES."

FEATURES!

"DAZED AT THE OFFER, I *TOOK* IT.

"AND THE FEATURES DID *BOFFO.*

"WHY, WHEN *FRANCIS THE TALKING MULE* CAME ALONG IN '49 -- THEY COULDN'T *TOUCH* US.

"STARS WERE *LINING UP* TO DO CAMEOS IN MY PICTURES -- THEIR KIDS WOULDN'T *LET* 'EM TURN US DOWN.

"I WAS THE *TOAST* OF THE TOWN. I WAS INVITED TO *ALL* THE RIGHT PARTIES, POPULAR WITH *WOMEN* --"

LEO, *DAAAAARLING!*

"-- IN THE *COLUMNS* ALL THE TIME --"

THIS WAY, KIDS! SAY '*SIRLOIN!*'

"IT WAS ALL ONE BIG MAD WHIRL OF *FLASHBULBS* AND *CHAMPAGNE.* I HAD IT GREAT, AND I *KNEW* IT --

"-- I HAD *EVERYTHING* --

"-- EVERYTHING I COULD EVER *WANT.*"

"AND THE *KIDS* SEEMED TO LIKE IT, AND IT KEPT A *ROOF* OVER MY HEAD --

"-- BUT THE MERRY-GO-ROUND RIDE WAS *OVER.* I GUESS I SHOULD HAVE BEEN HAPPY IT LASTED AS LONG AS IT *DID.*

"BEFORE YOU KNEW IT, PEOPLE I THOUGHT WERE MY *BOSOM BUDDIES* WEREN'T HOME WHEN I CALLED --

"-- AND THEY NEVER GOT AROUND TO *CALLING BACK* --

"-- AND FOR THE FIRST TIME, I HAD TIME TO *THINK* -- TO REALIZE HOW LITTLE I HAD.

"I WASN'T *ALIVE* UNTIL '46, BUT I WAS BORN WITH THE MEMORIES OF THE *CARTOONS* I'D BEEN IN --

"-- OF THE *ADVENTURES,* OF CHASTE ROMANCE WITH *LIONESS LOLA* --

"-- OF MY *RASCALLY NEPHEWS* --

"BUT ALL THEY WERE WERE *MEMORIES* --

"-- AND *FICTIONAL* ONES, AT THAT.

"I GOT INTO *TROUBLE* AFTER THAT -- *DRINKING* TOO MUCH, LOOSE WOMEN IN *BARS* --

"-- JUST GENERALLY *MIXING* IT UP.

"THE COPS SWEPT IT UNDER THE *RUG*, THOUGH --

"-- THEY *DID* THAT FOR CELEBRITIES IN THOSE DAYS. EVEN *HAS-BEENS.*"

SLEEP IT *OFF*, WOULDJA, MR. LEO? MY BOY WATCHES YOUR *SHOW* --

-- AN' I WOULDN'T WANT HIM T'BE *DISAPPOINTED.*

YOUR *BOY*, OFFICER?

WOULD HE LIKE AN *AUTOGRAPH?*

"STILL, THERE WASN'T A RUG *BIG ENOUGH* TO SWEEP IT UNDER WHEN *CORLISS McBRIDE* DIED.

"OH, *I* DIDN'T KILL HER -- NOT DIRECTLY, ANYWAY. SHE WAS A *HOOKER* --

"-- SHE OD'D IN THE *MOONGLOW*, A CHEAP HOTEL THAT WAS MORE *BORDELLO* AND *BAR* THAN ANYTHING ELSE.

"THE MOONGLOW WAS PRACTICALLY MY *SECOND HOME* BACK THEN -- AND CORLISS, WHO I KNEW AS *TRIXIE* --

"-- SHE WAS THE CLOSEST THING I HAD TO A *FRIEND.*

"AND EVEN *SHE* WOULDN'T'VE HUNG AROUND, IF NOT FOR THE *MONEY* I GAVE HER, AND THE DOPE SHE *BOUGHT* WITH IT."

Oh, AND IT TURNED OUT LITTLE CORLISS HAD A *SECRET.*

SHE WAS *FOURTEEN* YEARS OLD.

"I WAS THE ONE WHO *FOUND* HER, AND THE POLICE LOOKED AT ME JUST LIKE *ANYONE ELSE.*

"BUT I *WASN'T* ANYONE ELSE, WAS I?

"THERE WAS A *SCANDAL.* IT WAS IN THE *PAPERS,* COAST TO COAST --

Los Angeles Times EXTRA

February 7, 1957

KIDDIE TV STAR INVOLVED IN TEENYBOPPER DRUG DEATH

"He Killed Her For His Depr... Plea...

"-- AND CORLISS'S *MOTHER* TURNED UP FROM OHIO, DEMANDING I BE PUT IN *JAIL.*

"THERE WAS A BOOK LATER -- IT SEEMS CORLISS'S DEAR MA *BEAT* HER, WHICH IS WHY SHE RAN OFF IN THE *FIRST PLACE* --

"-- BUT THAT DIDN'T *MATTER* BACK THEN. IT MADE GOOD *HEADLINES,* IS WHAT MATTERED.

SHE WAS A *GOOD KID,* TRIXIE. I LIKE TO THINK IF I'D KNOWN, I COULD HAVE *DONE* SOMETHING, *HELPED* MAYBE.

BUT THAT'S A *CROCK.* MAYBE I DIDN'T KILL HER, BUT I SURE *HELPED* PUT THAT NEEDLE IN HER ARM --

-- AND WOULD IT *REALLY* HAVE MADE IT BETTER IF SHE WAS AN *EIGHTEEN-YEAR-OLD* JUNKIE CORPSE?

"THE GRAND JURY DECIDED NOT TO *INDICT* ME.

"NO EVIDENCE THAT *ANYONE* IN THE MOONGLOW HAD DONE WORSE THAN LOOK THE *OTHER WAY* --

"-- WHICH IS *BAD ENOUGH*, COME TO THAT. JUST NOT *ILLEGAL*.

"MY *CAREER*, OF COURSE, WAS AS DEAD AS *SHE* WAS.

"NOBODY WANTED AN ACCUSED *CHILD-KILLER* HOSTING A KIDDIE SHOW, AND WHO COULD *BLAME* THEM?

"AND THERE WAS *SOMETHING ELSE*, TOO.

"THERE WAS SOMETHING IN PEOPLE'S *EYES*, WHEN THEY LOOKED AT ME, SOMETHING *NEW*.

"IT WAS SOMETHING *HARSH*, AND COLD --

"-- AND IT WAS SOMETHING I'D *EARNED*.

"SO OUT I WENT, *AWAY* FROM IT ALL, AWAY FROM *EVERYTHING*.

"SO LONG, *HOLLYWOOD*.

"THERE'S AN *ADVANTAGE* TO BEING A CARTOON CHARACTER, ONE I'D NEVER *DISCOVERED* UNTIL THEN."

"MAYBE YOU GET *HUNGRY,* BUT YOU DON'T *NEED* TO *EAT,* NOT REALLY."

"SLEEP IN THE *RAIN,* FREEZE IN THE *COLD,* WALK THIS COUNTRY FROM *ONE* END TO THE *OTHER* --"

"-- YOU WON'T *DIE.*"

"NOT EVEN IF YOU DO IT FOR *SIX YEARS* -- IF NO ONE'LL HIRE YOU EVEN TO *WASH DISHES.*"

"I BEGAN TO PRAY FOR *DEATH,* FOR RELEASE FROM THE GNAWING EMPTINESS, THE COLD, THE *PAIN.*"

"BUT IT DIDN'T *COME.*"

"I WAS HUDDLED ON A CLIFF IN THE ROCKIES, WONDERING IF *WILD ANIMALS* COULD TEAR ME APART OR SOMETHING --"

"-- WONDERING IF EVEN *THAT* WOULD END IT --"

"-- WHEN *ZZARDO* FOUND ME."

I'M NOT PROUD OF WHAT HAPPENED *NEXT*. WELL, I'M NOT PROUD OF *MUCH*, ACTUALLY --

-- BUT AT LEAST *THIS* TIME, NOBODY *DIED*.

"YOU REMEMBER BACK IN '64, WHEN *HONOR GUARD* FOUGHT THE *MYTH-MASTER?*

"NO, YOU PROBABLY *DON'T* -- IT WAS BEFORE YOU WERE BORN, AND THE MYTH-MASTER NEVER *RETURNED*.

"HE WAS AN ARMORED FELLA. HE FOUGHT THE *SILVER AGENT*, THE *MERMAID*, *EL HOMBRE*, *CLEOPATRA*, *MIRAGE*, THE *HUMMINGBIRD* AND THE *N-FORCER* --"

HA! YOU MAY BE THE CHAMPIONS OF TODAY, HONOR GUARD --

-- BUT EVEN YOU CAN'T DEFEAT THE CHAMPIONS OF THE IMAGINATION!

"-- CONJURING FIGURES OF *FICTION* AND *FOLKLORE* TO BATTLE THEM.

"HE *BEAT* THEM, TOO -- EVEN THE SILVER AGENT COULDN'T WITHSTAND BOTH ACHILLES AND D'ARTAGNAN --

"-- BUT WHEN IT CAME TIME TO *KILL* THEM --"

CAN YOU FEEL IT, HEROES? CAN YOU FEEL REALITY DRAINING AWAY, AS YOU BECOME INSUBSTANTIAL --

-- NO MORE THAN BRIGHTLY-COLORED FANTASIES OUT OF SOME *COMIC-BOOK?*

ALL I NEED DO NOW IS THROW THIS SWITCH, AND --

-- AND --

"-- HE COULDN'T DO IT."

-- NO --

-- NO, I CAN'T --

"YOU COULD CHECK IT OUT -- THE STORY MADE THE PAPERS, LIKE THEIR CASES *USUALLY* DID.

"BUT WHAT *DIDN'T* MAKE THE PAPERS -- ASIDE FROM THE MYTH-MASTER TELLING THEM WHERE TO FIND *ZZARDO* --

"-- WAS THAT THE *MYTH-MASTER*, AS YOU'VE PROBABLY GUESSED --

"-- WAS ME."

"ZZARDO HAD TOLD ME I WAS A 'BELIEF-FOCUS,' THAT I SOAKED UP PSYCHIC ENERGY JUST BY *EXISTING.*

"HE WAS LYING ABOUT THAT *SECOND* PART, OF COURSE. HE JUST WANTED ME TO KILL *HONOR GUARD* FOR HIM. NOT THAT IT *MATTERED.*

"HE SAID I COULD *DRAIN* IT AWAY -- *KILLING* ME, SENDING ME BACK WHERE I *BELONGED,* WHATEVER.

"I DID THE *DIALOGUE* OKAY, BUT I COULDN'T PLAY THE *ROLE,* NOT FULLY. SO EVEN IF HE'D BEEN TELLING THE *TRUTH,* IT WOULDN'T HAVE HAPPENED.

"THE SILVER AGENT AND THE OTHERS WERE *SYMPATHETIC,* BUT STILL, THERE WAS GOING TO BE A *TRIAL* --

"-- UNTIL MY OLD PALS AT THE *STUDIO* STEPPED IN, THAT IS.

"FAGO'S FUNNY FEATURES WAS A PART OF *OMNIVERSAL PICTURES,* BY THEN --

"-- AND THEY'D BEEN MAKING GOOD MONEY WITH THEIR CARTOONS ON *TV* -- RERUNS, LICENSING, THE *WORKS.*

"EVERYTHING BUT THE *LOONY LEO* SHORTS, THAT IS. AND THEY WANTED TO SHOW *THOSE,* TOO --

"-- WANTED TO BRING 'EM OUT AS SOON AS PEOPLE HAD *FORGOTTEN* ABOUT CORLISS McBRIDE --

"-- AND THEY DIDN'T WANT *ANOTHER* SCANDAL DREDGING IT UP *ALL OVER* AGAIN.

"HONOR GUARD WAS WILLING TO GIVE ME ANOTHER *CHANCE,* AND SOME MONEY CROSSED THE RIGHT *PALMS* IN OUR FINE JUSTICE SYSTEM --

"-- AND LIKE *THAT,* IT ALL WENT AWAY.

"SOME MONEY CROSSED *MY* PAW, TOO. THE STUDIO DIDN'T WANT ME TURNING UP IN THE *PAPERS*, AFTER ALL --

"-- DIDN'T WANT ONE OF THEIR STARS TO SURFACE AS A *HOMELESS BUM.*

"SO THEY SET ME UP WITH A *STAKE*, AND IT WAS ENOUGH TO KEEP ME *GOING*.

"I BOUGHT A HOUSE IN *GOLDWATER HEIGHTS*, ON THE OUTSKIRTS OF *ASTRO CITY* --

"-- AND I DIDN'T GO *OUT* MUCH.

HOUSE FOR SALE

"THE HOUSE WAS EVENTUALLY THOUGHT TO BE *HAUNTED*, AND WHEN I *DID* GO OUT... IT WASN'T PLEASANT."

YAHH!
YAHH!

"THE KIDS HAD NO IDEA WHO I *WAS*, OF COURSE --

"-- THEY WERE JUST TERRORIZING THE NEIGHBORHOOD *FREAK.*

"AND THEN, IN *1976*, THEY STARTED SHOWING MY CARTOONS ON *TV* AGAIN. THE PAST, IT SEEMED, WAS FINALLY *PAST*.

"I WOULD *WATCH* THEM, AND TELL MYSELF THAT PART OF MY LIFE WAS OVER, AND THAT I WAS *BETTER OFF* FOR IT.

"BUT A FEW YEARS *LATER*, I WAS APPROACHED BY SOME BUSINESSMEN. *ENTREPRENEURS*.

"THEY'D TRACKED ME DOWN, FOUND OUT WHERE I *LIVED*.

"THEY WANTED TO OPEN A *RESTAURANT*, A FORTIES NOSTALGIA PLACE. AND THEY WANTED TO BUILD IT AROUND *ME* --

"-- TO MAKE ME A LIVING *PROMOTIONAL GIMMICK*.

"THEY LAID IT ALL *OUT* FOR ME, HOW IT WOULD *WORK*.

"THERE WAS ONLY ONE *HITCH*..."

WE NEED YOU TO BUY IN AS *PARTNER*. TO BE PART *OWNER* OF THE PLACE. IT'S PART OF THE *CONCEPT*, YOU KNOW?

LOONY LEO'S RESTAURANT -- IT'S A BETTER HOOK THAN LOONY LEO WORKING *IN* A RESTAURANT, RIGHT?

"LOOKING BACK ON IT, I WONDER IF THEY JUST DIDN'T HAVE ENOUGH MONEY *THEMSELVES*.

"BUT AT THE TIME, I WAS JUST *SCARED*. GOING OUT, FACING THE *PUBLIC* AGAIN --

"-- AND IF IT FAILED, I'D HAVE LOST MY STAKE -- I'D BE OUT ON THE *STREET* AGAIN --

191

"BUT STILL -- BUT *STILL* --

"ANYWAY, IT'S BEEN...*OKAY*.

"I LIVE UPSTAIRS, I WATCH THE *FOOD COSTS*, AND I MAKE SURE THE BARTENDERS POUR A DECENT *DRINK*.

"I COME OUT EVERY NIGHT, AND I PLAY MY PART AS *HOST* -- INTRODUCING THE *PIANO PLAYER* --"

GOOD EVENING, FOLKS, AND *WELCOME* TO LEO'S. THIS *ISN'T* DOOLEY WILSON AT THE PIANO, AND AS YOU'VE PROBABLY *NOTICED* -- -- *I'M* NOT HUMPHREY BOGART.

HA HA HA HA HA HA HA

"-- MINGLING WITH THE *CUSTOMERS*, ASKING IF THEIR FOOD'S GOOD, SIGNING *AUTOGRAPHS* --

"THE KIDS *LOVE* IT. AND THE ADULTS -- THEY SEEM TO LIKE THE SHEER *WEIRDNESS* OF IT.

"THEY COME *BACK*, ANYWAY.

"AND AT THE END OF THE *NIGHT* -- AT THE END OF THE NIGHT, EVERYONE'S *GONE* --

"-- SO I GO BACK UPSTAIRS AND I WATCH *OLD MOVIES* AND WAIT TO DO IT AGAIN *TOMORROW.*

"IT *WORKS.* IT FILLS THE *DAYS.*"

AND NOW HERE *YOU* ARE. YOU WANT ME BACK ON *TV.*

YOU WANT ME DOING COMMERCIALS FOR -- WHAT WAS IT, A *GARAGE?*

Ah, A CAR DEALERSHIP.

AND YOU CAN STILL SIT THERE AND *ASK* ME THAT, AFTER ALL I'VE *TOLD* YOU?!

193

WELL, AH, IT'S UP TO YOU, OF COURSE.

THE KIDS WHO GREW UP ON YOUR CARTOONS IN THE EIGHTIES ARE OLD ENOUGH TO BUY CARS NOW --

-- AND OUR RESEARCH SHOWS THAT THE NOSTALGIA APPEAL OF A CHILDHOOD FIGURE -- WELL, IT MIGHT BRING 'EM IN.

BUT IF YOU'RE NOT COMFORTABLE WITH IT, I'VE GOT A COUPLE OF BASEBALL PLAYERS I CAN TALK TO --

-- AND CHARLIE PROVOST, WHO USED TO BE STARFIGHTER'S SIDEKICK QUARK...

WAIT.

AH, WHAT THE HELL. IT'S SHOW BUSINESS, RIGHT?

SHOW ME THE PAPERS -- WHERE DO I SIGN?

YOU ARE NOW LEAVING ASTRO CITY PLEASE DRIVE CAREFULLY

Snapshots

One of the most enjoyable parts of creating a city is filling it with people. Whether they're heroes or villains, fantasy creatures or ordinary people, they've got to be engaging, distinctive, expressive and memorable. And luckily, working with artists of the caliber of Brent and Alex makes it easy to achieve those goals, no matter what I might throw at them. Herewith, some examples...
— KURT BUSIEK

Previous Page: Alex's design for Julius "Uncle Julie" Furst, the William Frawley of the First Family.

Air Ace has only appeared as a statue so far, but even a statue's got to be designed fully — and when you know the guy's going to show up in his own story someday, he's got to be designed carefully as well. For Air Ace, we wanted to combine a classic WWI pilot's look with just enough superhero elements to make him a believable bridge between a pulp hero and a superhero. The emblem on his chest and the wings on his goggles supplied just the right touch.

Thunderhead

It's one thing to say "a gigantic, threatening stormgod made entirely of dark clouds," and another to pull it off. To find the right look for Thunderhead, Alex was inspired by the "Night on Bald Mountain" section of Fantasia, and classical images of the Greek god Zeus. From Alex's original sketch, shown here, Brent developed the final rendition seen in "Welcome to Astro City."

HE SHOULD BE ABOUT THIS LARGE IN COMPARISON TO THE CITY.

It was easy to make Astra believable as a superhero, but we knew the story would hinge on how believable she was as a little girl. Alex did these sketches to capture her youth and innocence in a variety of moods.

The trick with Mister Smartie, Astra's computer-generated schoolteacher, was to make him expressive enough to be a character, while simple enough to look like a hologram. As you can see, Brent's early sketches included hair and detailed eyebrows, but the brows were simplified and the hair eliminated in the finished version, to make him more of an abstraction.

'MR SMARTY'
ACITY #2
VOL II
8-4-96

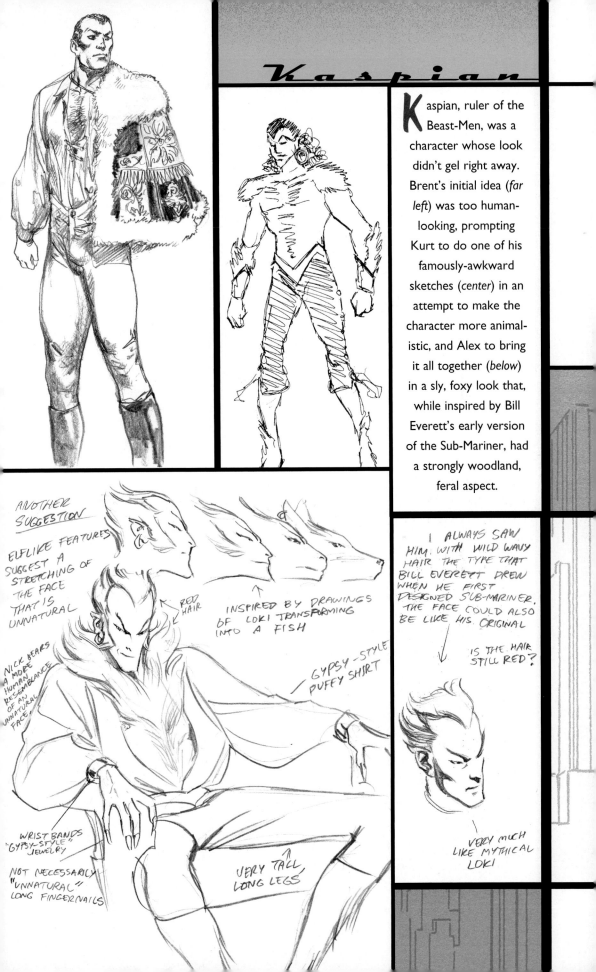

Kaspian

Kaspian, ruler of the Beast-Men, was a character whose look didn't gel right away. Brent's initial idea (*far left*) was too human-looking, prompting Kurt to do one of his famously-awkward sketches (*center*) in an attempt to make the character more animal-istic, and Alex to bring it all together (*below*) in a sly, foxy look that, while inspired by Bill Everett's early version of the Sub-Mariner, had a strongly woodland, feral aspect.

ANOTHER SUGGESTION

ELFLIKE FEATURES SUGGEST A STRETCHING OF THE FACE THAT IS UNNATURAL

NICK BEARS A MORE HUMAN RESEMBLANCE OF AN UNNATURAL FACE

RED HAIR

INSPIRED BY DRAWINGS OF LOKI TRANSFORMING INTO A FISH

GYPSY-STYLE PUFFY SHIRT

WRIST BANDS "GYPSY-STYLE" JEWELRY

NOT NECESSARILY "UNNATURAL" LONG FINGERNAILS

VERY TALL, LONG LEGS

I ALWAYS SAW HIM WITH WILD WAVY HAIR THE TYPE THAT BILL EVERETT DREW WHEN HE FIRST DESIGNED SUB-MARINER. THE FACE COULD ALSO BE LIKE HIS ORIGINAL

IS THE HAIR STILL RED?

VERY MUCH LIKE MYTHICAL LOKI

Include Mauser w/ light bulb

Hyper Sonic blaster

cordage reel

Coil of Rubber strapping
Spool of metal wire

- L'eggs egg "potato masher" grenades

Gold broque Holding a Laser/welder cannister

Modified hedge trimmer. (Diamond or molecular edged blades)

Multi-wave Flash gun

For the Junkman, we wanted someone who looked more cranky than dangerous, but who would nevertheless be striking and memorable, and whose gadgetry would be complex and fascinating. The Uncle-Sam beard was Alex's idea (wonder where he got that, hmm?), and the vacuum-cleaner jetpack was Brent's addition. The Mauser with the light bulb was Kurt's contribution, inspired half by a dummy raygun he saw at a convention, and half by Gyro Gearloose's bulb-headed "Helper."

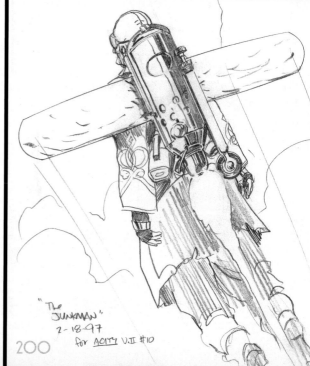

"The Junkman"
2-18-97
for ACITY V.II #10

As with Air Ace, we wanted the Black Rapier to look simple and elegant, and a fencer's costume seemed to be the obvious design choice. But the result was too plain, too ordinary-looking, until Alex gave him the combination sash/cape. A minor element, but it was just enough to make him a superhero, rather than simply a fencer with a different-colored outfit.

Jack-In-The-Box's alternate-future sons, The Box and Jackson, represented different design challenges, since unlike most of Astro City's denizens, we didn't want them to look classic or elegant. Instead, we wanted to evoke modern grotesqueries like Cable, Venom and Lobo — but still with a strong family resemblance to their progenitor. Kurt decided that one of them would be an organic monster, and the other a technological one — and Alex took that to heart, delivering a Jackson that featured Jack-In-The-Box's costume elements merged with his own flesh and distorting the human shape beneath, and a Box who'd been mutilated, his body augmented with clunky, functional-but-ugly additions. Justice Jacky was an inspired addition by Alex.

THE "ORGANIC" SON IS A VENOM/SABERTOOTH/ WOLVERINE TYPE

RED HAIR IN BOZO - WOLVERINE STYLE. MASK SHOWS ALL EXPRESSION LINE AND VEINS!

WHITE FACE & NECK

YELLOW EYES AND TEETH

TEETH GO ALL THE WAY BACK UP THE CUT OF MASK ... IF IT IS A MASK.

BLACK SKIN EXPOSED ON CHEST AND LEGS

ALL MUSCLES WELL DEFINED WITH THE COSTUME DETAILS

BIONIC IMPLANTS

JACK IN THE BOX ARM REPLACEMENT

RED & GREEN STRIPED SHORTS

BIONIC EYE

NO COSTUME WRINKLES

A BLACK MAN WITH WHITE MAKEUP JUST OVER HIS HEAD

RED LIPS

STILT MAN STYLE REPLACEMENT LEGS

INSTEAD OF A PROSTHETIC HAND, THERE IS A MECHANICAL PUPPET WITH KNIVES.

JACK - N' - BOX!

Zachary

Zachary Johnson, the face behind the mask of Jack-In-The-Box, was the emotional center of "Serpent's Teeth" and "Father's Day," and as such had to be a good enough "actor" to pull the story off. Here, Brent works with Zack's face to make him lively and expressive, while keeping him clearly Zack.

The first conception of Leo was as a cartoon lion in a tux, but something about it didn't seem right. We knew his story was one of disappointment and disgrace, and this dapper fellow didn't seem like he had the range for it.

Below: Expression studies, looking for a way to give Leo the right "hangdog" look. *Below right:* Figure proportion sketches.

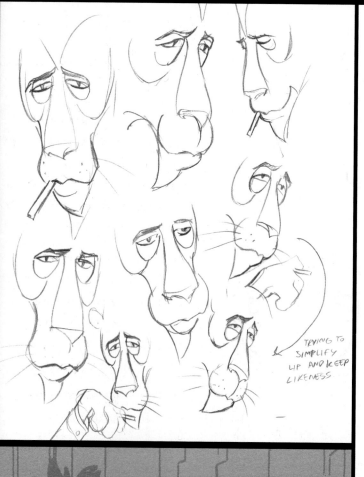

TRYING TO SIMPLIFY LIP AND KEEP LIKENESS

less torso

Bogart eyes

One hand almost always in pocket

smokes in "real" life (in deference to the late Joe Camel)

The key to Leo came in thinking of him as a leonine version of Humphrey Bogart in *Casablanca*. The white tux seemed to bring him into this century, and make him a lion of the people, not an elitist snob. Still, something wasn't clicking...

...until he got an abstraction of Bogart's lidded, weary eyes, and his "reality" level was cranked back far enough to make him look like a cartoon among humans, and not just an anthropomorphized jungle beast.

Left: That's a guy who can be a world-weary cartoon!

Alex's design for the Gentleman, the sartorially-impeccable fellow who's been performing well-mannered feats of derring-do in Astro City for coming up on six decades now. He hasn't had much of a chance at the spotlight yet, but he's got quite a history, and quite a story to tell.

And that's the frustrating thing about filling an entire city with such a host of characters. They all have stories — but they've got to wait their turn. So many characters, so few pages...

Cover Gallery

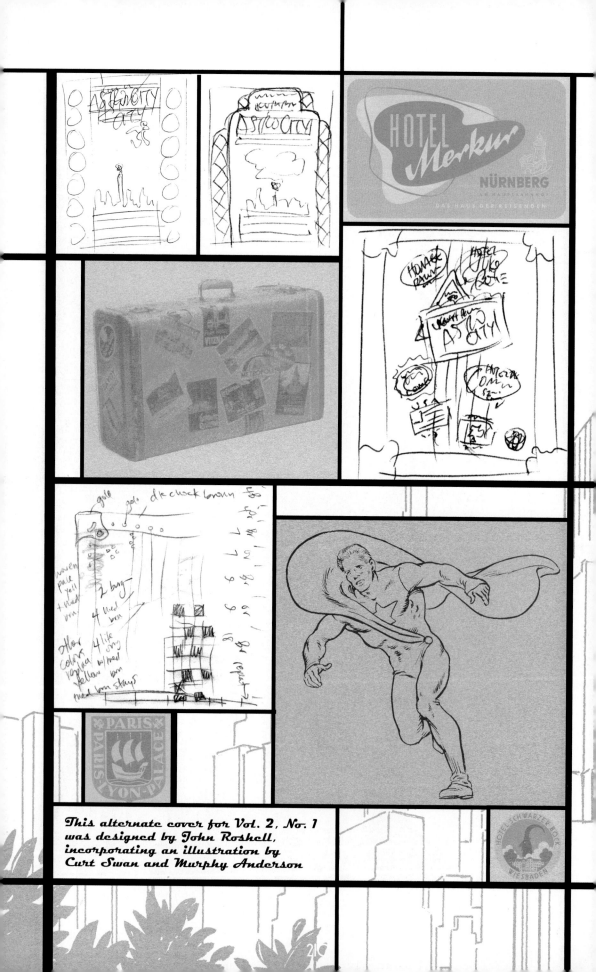

This alternate cover for Vol. 2, No. 1
was designed by John Roshell,
incorporating an illustration by
Curt Swan and Murphy Anderson

THE JUNK MAN

CYBORG WEARS
OLD 20'S STYLE
SWIM TRUNKS
RED & GREEN STRIPED

GET HUMPHREY BOGART REF!

CHANGE GUYS JACKET TO NORMAL MORE CASUAL "HE'S A MODERN GUY"